Think Yourself Slim
....changing your thoughts
to change your weight

by
Dr. Julie Coffey

Copyright © Julie Coffey 2017

All rights reserved. The author asserts their moral right under the Copyright, Designs and Patents Act 1988 to be identified as the author of this work.

Published by The Solopreneur Publishing Company Ltd
Illustrations provided by Stephanie Cooke (luckystepho@aol.com)
Except for the quotation of small passages for the purposes of criticism and review, no part of this publication may be reproduced, stored in a retrieval system, or transmitted, in any form or by any means, electronic, mechanical, photocopying, recording or otherwise, except under the terms of the Copyright, Designs and Patents Act 1988 without the prior consent of the publisher at the address above.

Medical Disclaimer
The information contained in this book is provided for education. It is not intended as, and should not be relied upon as, medical advice. The publisher and author are not responsible for any specific health needs that may require medical supervision. If you have any underlying health problems or have any doubts about the advice contained in this book, you should contact a qualified medical, dietary, or other appropriate professional.

The Solopreneur Publishing Company Ltd focuses on the needs of each individual author client. This book has been published through their 'Solopreneur Self-Publishing (SSP)' brand that enables authors to have complete control over their finished book while utilising the expert advice and services usually reserved for traditionally published print, in order to produce an attractive, engaging, quality product. Please note, however, that final editorial decisions and approval rested with the author. The publisher takes no responsibility for the accuracy of the content.

ISBN 978-0-9956591-8-6

Dedicated to ...
my treasured friends at Hot Yoga Sheffield

Contents

Acknowledgements

Getting The Most Out Of This Book

Introduction

Part 1 – This Is Why You Haven't Lost Your Weight Yet

1. The Cycle of Change
2. The Key to Successful Change
3. Two Parts of Your Mind
4. Subconscious Power vs. Will Power in the Battle to Lose Weight
5. Your Subconscious Is Always Listening
6. Even More Self Sabotage

Part 2 – Changing Your Thoughts To Lose Your Weight

7. Accepting Where You Are
8. What Do You Want?
9. The Reticular Activating System
10. You Can't Hit Anything Unless You Take Aim
11. The 'How To' Is Not Important At The Beginning
12. Getting Clear About What You Want
13. The 'How To' Lose Weight

Part 3 - 6 Steps to Personal Change and Weight Loss
14. There Is Something You Want
15. Forget The 'How To' And Dream Your Dream
16. Changing Your Belief
17. If You're Low You Need To Get Happier
18. Adding Power Every Day To Your New Program
19. Making A Plan

Closing Thoughts - It's Time To Stop Procrastinating And Make Yourself Worth It

About Dr. Julie Coffey and Uber Health Blog

Notes

Acknowledgements

Special thanks and love go to the Coffeys who have been there for me in a very difficult year. Thanks to my Mum, to my sister Helen, my brother Richard, and my lovely nephew Wade.

I offer enormous thanks and affection to my wonderful friends (you know who you are) who have also been there for me, you really have no idea how much you have helped and inspired me.

Thank you to Lulu my crazy greyhound for making me smile every day.

Thanks to Steph for providing the illustrations once again (luckystepho@aol.com)

Getting The Most Out Of This Book

This is a comparatively short book compared to my first book 'Living the Slim Life', but having put all of the information into practice myself very recently I KNOW just how powerful and life changing the stuff in here is, IF you use it rather than just reading about it.

Just reading this book will give you some understanding of new ideas, but reading alone will not facilitate change and you won't lose your weight.

When I was going through my own journey, I wrote a lot down in a journal so I could track my progress and see that how much ground I was covering. This will be helpful for you to do because at times you may feel like you haven't achieved anything. A quick flick through the notes you've written as you're going along serves as a great boost when you see just how much you have been doing.

A notebook is a great way of doing it, but there are a few blank pages at the end of this book to jot things down if that works better for you.

You won't be able to absorb everything in this book with just a quick read through. It will help you to make your own notes and think about how the contents of this book are relevant to you. This will help you to think about the changes you're going to need to make to lose your weight.

Whilst I hope you enjoy reading this book it's not really for your entertainment. I want it to change you so you can finally lose your weight and keep it off. The goal is for you to never have to do a diet again!

If you've got the hard copy of this book, a highlighter is a good idea. That way you can highlight the bits that really make you sit up and think – this will help focus your mind where it needs to be focused. You could write your thoughts and comments in the margins, or if you have any questions, you're welcome to email me.

To email me with your questions, feedback, and comments: drjulie@uberhealthblog.com

Introduction

"What would happen to your body if we could put our yoga teacher's mind into your head?"

"I'd lose loads of weight really fast!" my friend said with a laugh.

I'm coaching my friend with her weight loss, and we've just started as I begin to write this book. Our yoga teacher is very slim, very toned, and very yogi-like. She is very health focused, and it shows really clearly in her body and glowing health.

My friend's answer came fast and without much conscious thought, clearly showing that she knows her problem is her mind-set around her weight. She didn't turn her attention away from my question by saying things like "Oh well that wouldn't work for me because…

- All my family are fat, I'm overweight because of my genes
- I've got big bones, I've always been big
- My metabolism is slow
- I can't exercise because of my painful joints
- I've been fat since I was I child, this is the way I am

- My thyroid is underactive
- I was just never meant to be thin
- You can't enjoy food and be slim, I love my food!"

Have any of these come out of your mouth before? Be honest, have you used any of these as your reason for not being able to lose your excess weight yet?

None of these were mentioned, I was relieved as that means half of my work is already done for me. My friend knows where her problem is, she just needs help to move beyond it.

You see most people know enough to be a lot healthier and slimmer than they currently are. *You know* that if you eat better and perhaps less, and move your body around more than you do now, and you do that consistently, you'll lose weight.

But you just don't do that!

Why?

Because your mind isn't programmed to do it yet.

But it can be, and that's what you're going to learn from this book.

Gail at The Solopreneur suggested it was time I wrote my second book and due to personal life events at the end of 2015, the obvious book for me to write was a book about mind-set.

I had toyed with the idea of looking at this area in more depth than I'd covered in Living the Slim Life, because when you develop a slim mind-set your body follows suit, without the misery of a diet. Then I was given a lesson of my own about how important and powerful a strong and *deliberately directed* mind-set is, as I was suddenly and unexpectedly given the opportunity to put what I knew about this fully into practice at a much deeper level than was usual for me.

My mind-set was generally pretty good because I'd already worked on it for some time, but this kind of thing is work in progress and I still had lots of things to learn. But at this particular time in my life, I needed to step up several gears, and fast, if I was going to get myself out of a hole I was beginning to fall into.

40 Days of Hell

Towards to end of 2015, my family lost my much-loved dad. It was absolutely awful, the worst emotional pain I've felt in my life (up to that point). Exactly one week later my beautiful and lovely nan passed away too. It was a surreal time and affected my family quite deeply.

40 days after losing my dad, my partner of 13 years walked out on me.

My recent 'worst emotional pain' escalated to a level that was almost unbearable.

At a time when I needed to give as well as receive family support, my family shrank again, dramatically this time. I was struggling to give support to my immediate family. All of a sudden my partner wasn't there, and as a result, I also lost the support of their family. The sense of abandonment at this particular time in my life felt extreme and bewildering.

It was a lot to deal with all at once and to say my mood got a bit low would be an understatement!

I was six weeks into this misery when I was with a friend who said to me "Well at least it can't get any worse Julie!" But at that moment I realised it could, only this time it would definitely be *me making it worse for myself*, because of what was happening with my mind.

My thoughts were totally focussed on what was happening – my loss and being abandoned at the worst possible time. I was a self-employed GP locum at the time and couldn't work, so I had little income, creating money worries too. Everything seemed depressing. Not only had everyday life changed, but the future I had envisaged had evaporated too.

My bereavement reaction was initially quite healthy I think. It just felt like something I was living and feeling my way through. But when my partner left I didn't know who or what I was crying for, and it didn't feel healthy anymore, it felt desperate, horrible and isolated at times.

I knew I was in danger of getting swept up with all my negative thoughts, perhaps sinking into a depression, losing my income as a result, and getting into a complete and utter mess.

I could really easily make this loads worse for myself. All I had to do was continue to think the thoughts I was thinking.

It was obvious to me I had a *decision* to make, it seemed like sink or swim time. Continue riding the train of 'poor me,' get depressed and lose even more, or decide what I wanted instead and make it happen.

I decided to invite my sister over to drink a bottle of champagne (ok more than one) with me while I decided what I wanted for my new life, and as the evening wore on I created a list of things I wanted. I knew I needed to do a lot more than just this, but this was my starting point to get better.

That prompted me to revise what I'd learned about mind-set, learn some more, and **put it into practice** (that's the important bit!). That's what I did, and within a further 6 weeks I was 80% healed. Not bad going considering I was at the lowest point I'd ever been at, but the stakes felt high and I had decided I was worth it.

It was hard at first, but because I was clear about what I wanted, and knew how to go about achieving it, momentum build fast and I began a fairly swift recovery.

The exact same techniques I used to pull myself out of a hole and find happiness again are the same ones that will give you a health driven mind-set that will enable you to lose your excess weight once and for all.

Change Your Body by Changing Your Thoughts

In medicine, we're still trained to view the body as only a physical machine. This is surprising given that we're all aware of the placebo effect in medical studies.

A placebo is viewed as a 'sugar pill' or pretend treatment. It doesn't have any active ingredients and shouldn't really work to make any difference at all. But it does make a difference.

For example in studies looking at the effectiveness of antidepressants – 32% of people's mood improved while taking a placebo. 50% of people improved on the drug, but it could be argued that there was an even higher placebo effect in this group. Antidepressants often cause side effects, suggesting to the person taking it, it is, in fact, a drug and not a sugar pill, therefore increasing the belief that it's going to work.

I find this study about surgery even more fascinating. Dr. Bruce Mosely was the lead author of a study about the effectiveness of orthopaedic surgery in

2002. The aim of this study was to prove that there is no placebo effect in surgery. How could there possibly be?

They took a group of people with severe knee pain and they were split into three groups. Two of these groups had standard treatment of either the joint being washed out or the cartilage been trimmed and tidied up. This was done by keyhole surgery. The third group was the placebo group and they had small incisions made to their knee to make it look like they'd had some kind of keyhole surgery like the other two groups, but in fact, they'd had nothing done.

The two groups that had received standard treatment – either the shaving of the cartilage or a washout of the joint, showed the same level of improvement.

However, the third group who'd not actually had anything done apart from incisions made in their skin matched the other two group's level of improvement!

So there is indeed a placebo effect in surgery, in this case – just as good as the real thing, amazing! It seems when people believe/know something is going to help them, it does.

This is a real testament to the incredible healing power of the body. What could this do for you if you knew how to harness it?

The other incredible thing is how the placebo effect is pretty much glossed over in modern medicine so we can focus on 'the real and tangible stuff' of drugs and surgery.

Outside medical studies plenty of 'weird' things happen too. Take walking across hot coals for example. Some people believe/know they can walk across without getting their feet burned and their feet don't burn. Others aren't so sure and end up injuring their feet. How do you explain that?

What's the basis of all of this?

It's energy, thought energy in these cases, and quantum physics sheds some light on this. I'm not delving deep into quantum physics in this book, but it's a fascinating area to learn about.

Contrary to how we're taught to view the body as a solely physical, biological thing, it is responsive to invisible energy from across the electromagnetic spectrum. Invisible energy waves do affect the physical body. Indeed they are even used in a very small area in medicine.

People with kidney stones are sometimes offered high-frequency ultrasound treatment. Ultrasound is waves of energy and these energy waves are directed at the stone which results in it breaking into small enough pieces that can be passed out of the body. This is similar to a singer reaching the right pitch of note to shatter glass, by using the sound energy waves of their voice.

Energy waves have physical effects on your body.

Your body responds to energy. Some ways are obvious, for example, you're completely familiar with light and sounds. These are just energy vibrations that your eyes and ears respond to. You can also feel heat from the sun.

You can see the effects of other invisible energy waves, just think of what happens to the food you put into a microwave.

Biological processes can be influenced and controlled by invisible energy forces, including thoughts.

Most humans these days are so dependent on spoken and written language that we've neglected our energy sensing communication system. Most of us are only peripherally aware of it and a lack of use causes it to shrink.

Not all people have lost this, though. Australian aborigines are still connected to their hyper-sensory capacity in their daily lives. For example, they can sense water buried deep beneath the sand. That's the kind of stuff we in the Western world tend to trash as rubbish, mainly because we don't understand it anymore and have become really disconnected from it.

Thoughts directly influence your body's physiology. Thought energy can activate or inhibit cell activity. Sometimes this is obvious and immediate. For example, when you think of a horrible thought that stresses you out, such as "I can't cope being on my own", the panic sets in. Or you see a person you really fancy and think "phwoar" and a smile spreads across your face. Or you deliberately think relaxing and calming thoughts and your body relaxes and slows down. All of this starts as a thought and has its effect on the body physically.

However, a lot of stuff is going on at a subconscious

level, which means it's below the level of your conscious awareness. You might be surprised to know that your conscious mind is in control of your life about 5% of the time, while the rest is in the hands of your subconscious.

Our lives and our results are basically a printout of our subconscious programming, including our health and weight. Subconscious programming operates without the necessity of observation or control of the conscious mind. We're often completely unaware that our subconscious minds are making our everyday decisions and basically running the show.

This book is about changing the subconscious programming that you currently have concerning your weight and health, because if you're reading this book what you've got running right now isn't serving you very well.

You can't reach into your subconscious mind and remove programs like you can with a computer, but you can write another one and lay it over the top, making the old one defunct.

Prepare to write another program and get what you want with your weight and health.

In the next part of this book, I'm going to explain exactly why you haven't lost your weight yet. Following on from that I'll explain how to lose your weight and keep it off, then I'll finish with some practical tools about how to pull all of this together to make it work for you.

Let's get started.

Part 1
This Is Why You Haven't Lost Your Weight Yet

Part 1
This Is Why You Haven't Lost Your Weight Yet

By the time you've finished reading this section of the book you're going to have a good idea as to why you haven't lost your weight yet. It's due to the obstacles you've unwittingly put in your own way. This section is going to put you in a new position so you can begin your weight loss in a different way. And after all, if you want something different to what you've currently got, you've got to do something different.

If you're like a lot of people, you've been struggling to achieve your desired weight for a long time. You've put in a great deal of effort, you may have spent a lot of money, but you still haven't cracked the problem.

You may have tried one diet after another. You might have lost a lot of weight, only to put it all back on again and possibly a bit more too. It's almost like you're attached to an elastic band, being dragged back to your starting point time and time again.

The diet industry has fuelled the 'quick fix' approach to weight loss by telling you what you should *do* in order to *have* what you want – weight loss. Depending on which diet you choose, you're told what to eat, what not to eat, and how much to eat. You might be told how much exercise you should be taking too.

The *'do this'* to *'have this'* approach just does not work for the vast majority of people when it comes to weight loss and that's because it misses who you have to actually be in order to **be** healthy, happy and slim.

Remember in the introduction when I told you about my question to my friend? She knew if she could transplant our yoga teacher's healthy mind-set into her head she would instantly be someone new when it came to her health and weight. She knew her excess weight would come off pretty much effortlessly because she would have changed.

The *'do this'* to *'have this'* approach requires willpower, which is a good enough reason all on its own for not working. It saddens me to hear people say the reason they're fat is that they haven't got any willpower when it comes to food and exercise. Successful weight loss isn't just about that. Trying to lose weight with will power is no fun at all and sets you up for a fall, disappointment and the feeling that you're simply not good enough – that's rubbish in fact.

Successful weight loss starts in the mind and not

with a prescriptive meal plan or prescribed exercise program. A good place to begin understanding this is knowing something about the cycle of change.

1. The Cycle of Change

Having an insight into the psychology of the cycle of change is a good way for me to introduce the most important ingredient to successful weight loss. It helps you to understand why you absolutely have to have a very clear idea of what you're aiming at, what you're setting your sights on, and what you really want from your effort if you intend to succeed with your weight loss.

This graph shows you how you can expect your mood to change as you undertake the journey of improving your health and losing your weight.

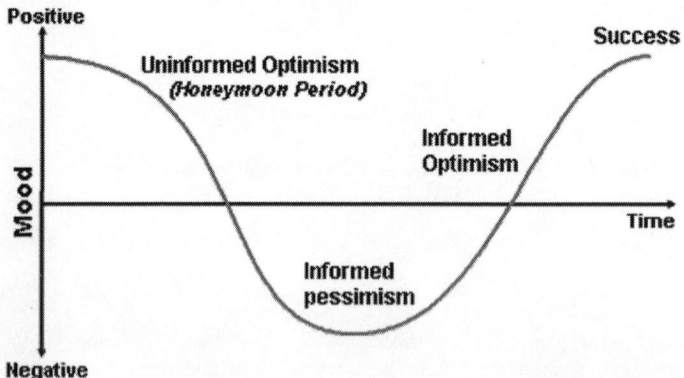

The first part of the cycle of change is often referred to as the honeymoon period. You've been at this place before and it's when you're at the beginning of a brand new diet. You might be there again now with reading this book.

You're optimistic, you're looking forward to losing loads of weight. The novelty might even make it seem fun at first! At this stage, you haven't fully appreciated what you need to do to achieve the results you're after. At this stage of the game, you are uninformed of the changes you'll need to make, and the cost involved to you.

This stage doesn't last very long, as you may well know. As soon as the reality of what you've got to do to achieve results hits you, you move onto the next bit of the cycle.

Pessimism.

Negative feelings start to creep in here as you learn more about of what's required of you to make this work.

Feeling negative and a bit down is entirely normal and to be expected during any process of change.
Perhaps this isn't going to be as easy as you thought! The benefits you imagined before you started with the diet and/or exercise plan seem a long way off. They might not even seem real and you begin to feel like

you may have been kidding yourself that you could change and achieve the amount of weight loss you had in mind.

The costs, i.e. sticking to a diet or a change in eating and exercising, are becoming apparent and it feels really difficult. It's certainly not fun! You ask yourself "is this worth it?" and look for reasons to stop.

Once you slip down to the bottom of the cycle there is a real risk of giving up. After all, you can end the discomfort of dieting right now by stopping it and going back to normal.

But this trough is normal. It is normal to have a low point when you are changing something about yourself. By knowing it's coming you can stack the odds in your favour to get you out the right side and not end up back at your starting point.

One thing that will get you out of this is trough is to remember the reason you started this in the first place – 'your aim'. Why did you start on this path? What is it that you want? How good does it make you feel when you think about it?

If you can think about where you're headed and

feel absolutely great about it because you're looking forward to it so much, you will be able to start climbing out of the trough and head in the direction of where you want to go. This is because you've got a great reason to overcome the inevitable difficulties you will encounter. Your reason will draw you towards your goal. Difficulties become things to work through, not things to send you back to where you started. Pessimism will then gradually change into something else.

Optimism.

For those who have a strong enough reason to keep going, you will start coming out of negativity. Chances of success are quite high now, but it's not a done deal yet. You know what you need to do and you're well informed about it now.

Your mood is getting better, you're seeing and feeling the benefits of the changes you've been making. The costs of change feel less because they are gradually becoming your new habits – they're just things that you do now, it's no big deal anymore.

The key here is not to stop, because the new habits aren't quite cemented yet. They need a bit longer to bed in for you to move into the next part of the cycle.

Success!

The last part of the cycle of change is success! You have got to where you've been aiming for.

You've made it, you're fully experiencing the benefits – you've lost weight and are feeling fantastic! The costs of doing so are now minimal because your changes have become a habit, which means they happen pretty easily, they have just become part of your routine. You have changed where it counts, in your mind.

When you change your mind, your body has to follow suit.

2. The Key to Successful Change
The absolute key to successful change is knowing what success is for you. Can you say in a sentence or two exactly what it is you want? You have to have a good enough reason if you're going to successfully take this journey. You need something great that's going to get you out of the trough because you will end up in there – that's normal.

I see people every day in my GP work who say they want to lose weight. An educated guess would say 1 in 25 will succeed and I usually spot the ones who will go on to do well by asking them to answer one question:

"Why do you want to lose weight?"

What does success look like for you?

Why do YOU want to lose weight? What is your reason why?

Whatever comes to mind jot it down here. The only wrong 'why' at this stage is the one you don't write down!

> Why do I want to lose weight?

There are no wrong answers at this stage and whatever it is you'll probably tweak it as you read further. But if you don't write anything down you've got nothing to work with and you can't take any steps forward from where you're sat right now at this very minute.

Write something about what you want. Do it now before you read any further.

I'm worried about you already if you don't write anything down, though!

Write something, anything, just write it! By doing this you are beginning to do something different – and after all, if you want a different result you've got to start doing things differently. Start doing it now, don't be sat here this time next year at the same weight as you are right now because you couldn't be bothered to think about what you want.

By thinking about what you want and writing

something down, you are beginning to engage the part of your mind that will turbo charge your efforts to lose your excess weight, without being stuck on some miserable diet.

Please don't skip this bit, otherwise you'll miss out on something that is going to help you to lose your weight.
Coming back to the answers I get from my patients and clients when I ask them what they want, there are generally two kinds of answers I tend to get.

"I want to be slimmer" The person with this answer has a 95% chance of failing. How is this going to get you out of the tough of misery on the cycle of change? It's not!

Compare that reason 'why' to this one:

"I imagine having the energy to walk to the top of Snowden and feel great! I see myself reaching the top and my wife giving me a lovely tight cuddle. I feel an immense sense achievement as I breathe in the clean, fresh air. I feel really pleased with myself when my wife tells me how proud she is of me."

The person who answers like this has already taken a

massive step towards successful weight loss because successful weight loss starts in the mind - it starts with a goal that you're emotionally connected to. That's the thing that will get you through the dip on the cycle of change, helping you to succeed.

How does your reason why compare to these two reasons? Do you need to think a bit more about what you really want? If you're like most people, you probably do!

Give it some more thought and have another go at writing down what you want, what you really want regarding your weight.

> Why do I want to lose weight?

This really is a big step in the reprogramming of your mind. You're taking a big step in the right direction.

Readers of my first book – Living the Slim Life – will know I am no fan of restrictive diets. So although I've used the word 'diet' while explaining the cycle of change, **I DO NOT** advise you to use the information in this book to help you stick to a restrictive diet.

I advise getting your mind-set sorted out first. If you're like most people, you already know how to eat a lot better than you're doing currently. You don't need to go on a diet, you know more than enough to make a big difference already. But there is something that is holding you back from putting what you know already into consistent practice – your current mind-set.

Once you're getting to grips with the information in this book, you may want to learn more about nutrition and that will be an important and helpful thing to do, especially if you've done a lot of dieting in the past. Because some of the nutritional information from the diet industry is very unhealthy and can actually help to keep you fat! But put good foundations down first (your mind-set), so your efforts don't come crashing down i.e. you gain all the weight you previously lost.

This book is about getting all parts of you engaged and working together in harmony towards the same outcome. It's about removing the self-sabotage which has been keeping you stuck on a never ending plateau, or yo-yoing up and down with your weight.

3. Two Parts of Your Mind
You probably know that you have two different parts to your mind, but you are only consciously aware of one of them – your conscious mind. You're not very often aware of what your subconscious is up to, but you can notice it, for example, when one of your buttons has been pressed.

You might know someone who has an annoying habit and as soon as they do this annoying thing you get irritated or mad. One minute you're fine and the next you're not. You're completely wound up or upset. Your button has been pressed and your subconscious plays the program you've got stored for that particular button.

You might be an emotional eater, maybe you eat in response to upset or stress. Something upsetting happens and before you know what's happening you're eating your way through the contents of your fridge. Basically, one of your buttons has been pressed, putting into action one of your stored programs. It feels as though you have no control over this!

You are using your conscious mind right now, as you read this. It's the part of your mind that's actively aware of things at any given moment. In addition to these words you're reading you may be aware of the birds singing outside, what the weather's doing, or like me – that you'll need to sit up straight soon or you'll get backache.

You also use your conscious mind to reason things out and to think, as you do when you're looking for a solution to a problem, or in the early stages of learning something new.

Cast your mind back to when you were learning to drive, you had to think about everything you did. It was a real effort at the start. But the more you practised, the less you had to think about what you were doing because it was becoming automatic. You were learning the skill of driving – which means you were literally programming the skill into the other part of your mind (your subconscious).

Once the driving program was installed into your subconscious mind (by the repeated focus of your conscious mind) you didn't have to think about driving anymore. You could just get in the car and drive, hardly thinking about it at all. Your subconscious is the BIG storehouse for your learned behaviour and habits.

Take learning to drive as an example. You can see that your subconscious mind can be compared to a hard drive on a computer – ready for programs to be loaded onto it. Your subconscious doesn't have a choice about the programs loaded onto it – the choice is down to you. And you make that choice by deciding what to direct your focus of attention to.

You make this choice - sometimes very deliberately, as in the case of driving. But more often, program installation into your subconscious happens by accident, rather than by the deliberate intention of learning to drive, walk and talk.

It often involves no plan or consideration of the consequences and happens by accident. Before you know it you have a behaviour that isn't helping you and it seems to have a life of its own – coming to life when certain buttons are pressed.

Take overeating, eating in response to upset, and doing very little exercise as examples. You weren't born like this. You learned this somewhere along the way. These are all learned behaviours that were repeated often enough sometime in the past to become embedded into your subconscious as habits. You weren't born with these 'bad habits', but somewhere in your past you successfully programmed them into your subconscious, and they became part of you.

At some point, you decided you wanted to learn to drive. You directed your conscious mind to focus on the task at hand. You stayed alert in your driving lessons and gradually learned how to drive.

You decided you wanted the 'driving program' installed into your head. You directed your conscious mind to practice the skill, which in turn got fed into your subconscious mind. Once your subconscious 'got it', which it does by repeated practice, your conscious mind could switch off from this task, and focus its attention on something new.

Compare your deliberate plan to learn to drive to this example:

You gave little or no conscious thought about whether it would be a really good idea (or not) to treat yourself to a big meal after a hard day's work (i.e. overeat). After all, you've been working hard, you deserve a reward! This is ok if it's every now and then and you're *thinking* about what you're doing and why you're doing it. For example, I may overeat if I go out for a meal because the food is lovely and I'm making the most of it and indulging. But this is an exception, not the general rule.

But when you're not really thinking beyond the 'I deserve this' and doing it after every hard day at work, it gradually becomes a regular thing. Gradually you begin to do it every evening because repeated actions are the key to creating habits. What started out as a reward for hard work quickly becomes an established habit (learned behaviour) and you're overeating on a regular basis, it becomes your new norm.

The more you do the same thing over and over again the more it becomes a habit – it ends up being just what you do. You put too much on your plate because you 'deserve it' and your cue to stop is an empty plate, not what your stomach is trying to tell you.

The same thing happens if you start using food to soothe your emotions, i.e. comfort-eat, rather than deal with them in a less destructive way. Repeatedly choosing the comfort of your sofa over doing a bit of exercise is another bad habit in the making. You're not born like this, but these bad habits become your normal because you practice them until they become automatic.

Before you know it (and you may not even notice, because habits are like that – they're operating below your consciousness once you've set them up) you're overeating at every meal time or responding to all stress by eating or always choosing to be sat down rather than being active.

These behaviours feel part of you. You may say "It's just the way I am!" No, it's not! It's only your current program and you can choose to create a different one.

Your initial set-up for overeating, emotional eating, or being sedentary maybe something completely different, but the process is the same.

Your subconscious mind is absolutely huge compared to your conscious mind. It's like a big hard drive that stores all your memories and all your learned behaviours and habits. Most things stored in your subconscious have been put there via your conscious mind either deliberately (like your learned skill of driving), or more commonly by accident (like your bad habits of eating too much, eating too many of the wrong things, doing too little exercise and all the other ones that are keeping you overweight).

Once a behaviour has been passed into your

subconscious mind, will power can't override it for very long, it is a very poor contest because the power difference is far too great. It is extremely difficult for the conscious mind to consistently override an established program within the subconscious mind. And this is exactly why diets do not work. It's not your fault. You are not weak-willed.

By going on a diet, you set yourself up for failure.

4. Subconscious Power vs Will Power in the Battle to Lose Weight
Think about this.

Most conscious thought uses some of your energy. At the beginning of your day you have a certain amount of energy and no more. It's a bit like how much petrol you have in your car. Even if it's full to maximum, it is still limited and you will run out at some point.

So let's say every conscious thought you have uses some energy. Think about the mental effort it took to learn how to drive when you first started. But your established behaviours and habits take hardly energy at all because anything that's been programmed into your subconscious literally runs on autopilot. The 'work' (accidently or deliberately) of putting it there has been done previously.

Think about the mental energy it takes to drive now (if you've been driving for years), compared to what it was like when you were learning. There's a big difference isn't there?

Most conscious thought uses some of your energy. Established habits within your subconscious use practically none and run on autopilot. Are you seeing where I'm going with this?

Before you read on, put your hands together, with your fingers interlinked. One of your thumbs will be on top. Now interlink them the other way, so the other thumb in on top.

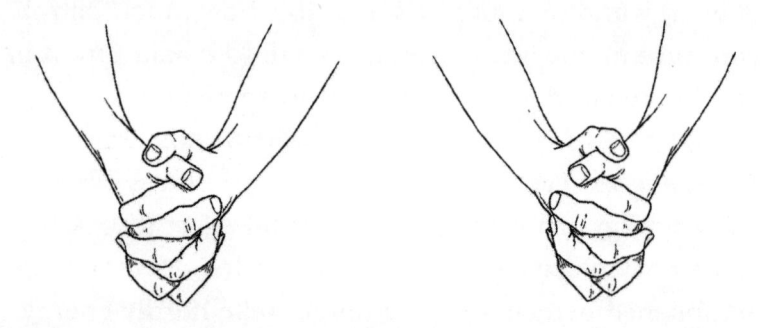

The first time you joined your hands together, it felt 'normal'. The second time you did it, it felt a bit funny didn't it, a bit strange and not quite right. That's because the first time you did it you were acting out of habit, you didn't think about it, you just did it. It felt comfortable and right.

The second time is not your habitual way of doing it, so it doesn't feel right. But not feeling right doesn't exactly make it wrong, does it?

Spend about thirty seconds going backward and forwards, interlinking your hands the 'right' way and then the 'wrong' way. Keep doing it fairly quickly.

You'll notice that the 'wrong' way becomes less 'wrong' the more you do it and feels much more comfortable. If you carried on doing this long enough you would become equally comfortable doing it either way. You'll have created a new habit.

Doing things that are contradictory to your established habits will feel odd, a bit weird, and even downright wrong. But this does not make the new action wrong - if you ever feel it does, do that little exercise with your hands to remind yourself!

Let's say you've got a tendency to have a latte and a piece of cake every time you go to your favourite café with your friend. You don't need to think about this, you've done it so many times it's just what you do! In fact, to do something different (for example not have the cake and choose a healthier drink) would feel odd and might actually feel quite wrong – like joining your hands together with the other less comfortable way. (Or maybe it makes you feel resentful of the diet you're on because that's the only reason you're doing it!)

But you're on a diet at the moment and so you feel

you can't have the latte and the cake. But, you've got an established habit of having a latte and cake! And that habit is running on autopilot, which means it has almost limitless energy, whereas the energy of your conscious mind is limited. As the battle plays out over time, who's going to win – limitless energy, or limited energy?

This is why you fall off the diet wagon. It was always going to happen. It was just a matter of time. You feel bad, but you shouldn't. A diet is the wrong tool for the job. It's like trying to use a hammer when you really need a screwdriver.

Getting healthy and losing weight requires you to take a different course of action instead of the action your current programs are programmed to take.

Diets can only work if you have enough willpower to consistently (i.e. pretty much all day every day) override your subconscious programming. Diets fail 95% of the time and that's because willpower is just no match what-so-ever for your subconscious, the odds are far too great.

You have to approach the situation in a different way. You have to literally write a new program and put it into your subconscious. When you do that, the old one naturally falls into disuse and over time becomes irrelevant. However, in the early days the new habit you want to develop may feel a bit odd and certainly less comfortable than the old one – just the same as having the 'wrong' thumb on top.

If you learned how to drive (or walk), it means you have the skill to program your subconscious with something new. And it doesn't matter how long ago these things were learned, or how old you are now, you can learn the skill of being slim and healthy. You can get this set-up, so it runs on autopilot. As easy as it is now to maintain your excess weight, it will become just as easy to achieve and maintain your ideal weight. You know people who do this don't you, we all know people who do this and it's all down to their programming.

5. Your Subconscious Is Always Listening

Your subconscious mind is really different to your conscious mind and it communicates in a totally different way to your conscious mind. You can know what you want, for example, "I want to be a size 10", but to make it happen you have to communicate that to your subconscious because it's your subconscious mind that will make it happen.

You use your conscious mind to think, reason and use lose logic. With your conscious mind, you differentiate between the past, the present and the future, and flit between the three.

You can embed things into your subconscious with repetition, like learning to drive or learning to play a musical instrument. Your subconscious mind also communicates with feelings. It doesn't communicate with words and language, although the words you use do create feelings which are passed through to your subconscious.

Your subconscious mind is totally focused on the present. The past and future don't exist for the subconscious, it works in the present. This is a knock back to primitive origins. The conscious mind is a much more recent and higher development. The subconscious is a great big storehouse and it's all about the here and now.

You know what it feels like when you get a gut feeling about something? That's your subconscious trying to get your conscious attention. For example, you might be about to make a decision about taking a new job, but have a bad gut feeling about it. That's your subconscious telling you that you need to look deeper because something's not right with the way things stand right now. Or pure and simple this isn't a good move for you at all, despite what it looks like on paper.

On the other hand, you might be ready to accept the new job. You feel excited and happy. That's your subconscious being in alignment with your conscious decision. You're in harmony with yourself – this is likely to be a great move for you.

Your subconscious communicates with feelings. This is where logical and reasoned goal setting, be it about your weight or anything else, can fall flat and not work very well at all.

If you're someone who already writes your goals and aspirations down, you're a step ahead of most people, because most people don't do that! So well done so far! However, reading the written words or just thinking about them will have little impact on your subconscious programming, unless you mix emotion in with it too – because that's what your subconscious mind understands best.

If you just think about being slimmer, but don't really have much emotion attached to that thought, it's hardly going to register with your subconscious at all. It will have little impact. Consciously you might know what you want, but you haven't communicated it with the part of your mind that can make it happen yet. It's like pressing down on the clutch peddle in your car, but the cable has broken. You won't communicate your intention to change gear with the engine and as a result, you're going nowhere.

You have to speak to your subconscious in its language, and my bet is you're already doing that very well indeed, just in the wrong way! Most people are already very good at sending completely the opposite message about what they actually want to their subconscious.

If you look at a photo of yourself and think "Oh my god, I look so fat!" and feel really, really bad and upset about it – well that's a perfect way to communicate with your subconscious that you want to stay fat! Because your subconscious understands emotions, not words. And the stronger the emotion you create, the louder the message. Your subconscious hears this message loud and clear!

You are focusing on something, in this case being fat. You have mixed lots of emotion with it, you feel sad and upset. Emotion is the key to take what you're focusing on straight into the subconscious, delivering the message that this is what you want (even if consciously it is the opposite).

So you are already very good at communicating with your subconscious, but you mostly do it by accident, without thought, and usually send the opposite message to what you actually want. Can you see how you're already pretty good at this!

Your subconscious is very powerful, but it is under the direction of your conscious mind and everyday thoughts. Once you understand this and make some changes, weight loss becomes an awful lot easier.

When you were *focussed* on learning to drive, your subconscious was all ears. By repetitive practice, it got the message loud and clear "I'm a driver" and the program was laid down. Repetition communicates with your subconscious.

Whatever you focus on, especially when there's emotion attached to it (happy or sad), it gets fed straight into your subconscious mind. The way your subconscious mind works means that what you focus on and give your attention to becomes important and relevant. It therefore expands, takes on a life of its own and you get more of it.

You focussed and gave your attention to learning to drive, you therefore became a driver.

When it comes to your health and weight, where is your predominant focus? What did you write down the very first time I asked you what you want? If your focus is mainly on where you're at right now (which for most people it is), it's one of the biggest reasons you're struggling to lose your weight. What is this repeated focus inviting into your life?

That's a very easy one to answer, because whatever you've been predominantly focussed on just lately is exactly what you will have right now.

If you're focussed on what you have now and are giving your predominant attention to your current weight (especially if you're feeling bad about it), you are doing a great job at staying exactly where you are, or perhaps putting even more weight on. Because what you focus on makes it relevant to your subconscious and if it's relevant it expands (compare with your waist and/or hips!).

If you're overweight, your predominant focus has been on being overweight. Although your subconscious is very powerful, it doesn't question your chosen focus, that's down to you. This focus by your conscious mind is getting fed into your subconscious mind, reinforcing what's already there.

I'd like you to write down 5 thoughts you commonly have about yourself regarding your weight and health.

---

5 things I commonly think about myself
-
-
-
-
-

If you think things like:
- I'm fat
- I hate my body
- I can't get into my clothes
- I'm miserable about my body
- Nothing ever works
- My knees hurt
- I've got no energy

If you feel bad and upset while thinking or saying these things, which you inevitably will, you are very effectively communicating to your powerful subconscious mind that you want to be fat (and all those other things). This is easy for your subconscious. It just needs to keep running the current program.

That's just the way it works! If only we had learned

this stuff as kids, imagine all the trouble we could have saved ourselves.

Repeated attention and focus (especially when mixed with emotion) makes the object of attention relevant to your subconscious. In the case of your weight, the job of your subconscious is easy – maintain the status quo, keep running the same program, no need to change direction.

Your subconscious is completely different to your conscious mind, but once you understand that you're on the brink of making some transformational changes.

Think about the thoughts you have on a day to day basis about your weight. Where is your focus? Most people have this completely backward because we were never given a manual about how to use our own hard drive at school – more's the pity.

Where's your focus, what are you inviting in?

The other important difference with your subconscious is that it doesn't differentiate between something real that is happening right now, and something vividly imagined in your mind right now as if it is happening.

Think about what happens to your heart rate if you're walking alone in the dark and you suddenly feel like you're being followed. Now think about what happens to your heart rate if your lovely family gives you a birthday present and it's a skydiving experience. You *imagine* doing it and it's really scary! (I know this feeling well because I've got to set a date to do this at the time of writing this bit and it's scaring the hell out of me!). As far as your subconscious is concerned the effect is the same, it doesn't matter that one is real and actually happening, and one is being imagined vividly in your head.

This is actually really useful when it comes to weight loss, because while you can't suddenly look in the mirror and see the body of your dreams, you can imagine it. And the more you imagine what you *really* want, *feel happy* about it, and the more you shift your focus towards what you want (and away from what you don't want), the more your subconscious will give you what you really want. How cool is that!

Remind yourself that your subconscious makes no differentiation between past, present or future. It's primarily the emotion that your thoughts *right now* at this moment trigger that your subconscious hears and responds to.

So if you're sitting there worrying about how fat you're going to look on the beach when you go on holiday, and feeling horrible about that – guess what? You're telling your subconscious you want to be fat. You're doing this with emotions that your thoughts have triggered. Your subconscious will oblige by doing what it does well, it will keep you overweight and you will find yourself constantly sabotaging yourself. You will be wondering why you seem to be your own worst enemy – and it's simply because the two parts of your mind are working contradictory to each other, and the stronger of the two will win every time.

Every thought about being overweight is reinforcing the program that is already there. Your thoughts up to this point have acted as a massive anchor in the ground preventing you losing weight. Or they have you on a bungee jump – you lose weight only to be yanked back to your starting point very quickly.

6. Even More Self Sabotage

Here is another very common way a lot of people inadvertently sabotage themselves and keep themselves overweight by reinforcing their current programming.

Have you ever looked at or pointed at a slim fit looking person and said: "Look at them, it's so easy for people like that, I hate people like that!" And feeling a real dislike for this person who you've never even met! In one way or another, or about one person or another, we've all done it.

What do you think your accepting and unchallenging subconscious mind makes of that?

If it could be put it into words it would be something like this.

'Skinny cow! I don't want to be like that! Why would I want to look like that and have people feel bad about me too? So I'll stay fat! I don't want to be a skinny person who people point at and hate! Good job I've got the 'fat program' running – I'll carry on with it.'

What your negative feeling about this slim person has done is strongly reinforce your current program of being overweight.

How many times have you indulged in 'fat chat' by chatting with friends or work colleagues about being overweight, about not being able to lose weight, about how awful the current diet is, how difficult it is to exercise, that you're not going to get into your wedding dress?

Where is your focus, where are your emotions when you do this? Every time you chose to engage in this kind of conversation you are reinforcing the 'stay fat' message to your subconscious. Your subconscious gives you what you focus on.

Are you a 'fat defender'? Have you ever defended why you haven't lost weight yet?

- I'm big because I'm big-boned

- I'm overweight because my thyroid is underactive
- All my family are overweight, it's because of my genes
- I've always been big, this is just the way I am

Every time you defend and justify your current position you are reinforcing that position and you're doing that by your continued focus on where you are now. In fact, you are strengthening your bond to where you are right now, by looking for explanations as to why you are there. The more explanations and reasons you find, the tighter the bond.

It's very, very difficult to move to a slimmer body while engaging with this kind of thought and conversation. Neither can you if you indulge in any excuses for not losing weight. Have you used any of these?

- I'm too busy to exercise
- I can't afford healthy food
- I haven't got time to prepare healthier food
- I'll never be slim so what's the point trying?
- It's hard to be healthy when your partner isn't doing it too
- I can't stick to a diet, so there's no point in starting
- I haven't got enough will power
- Life it too difficult right now

Defending and making excuses also creates negative emotion, communicating your current point of focus very powerfully to your subconscious.

These are some of the ways that overweight people continually keep their focus on all the things they don't want. This sends a clear message to your subconscious that this is what you do want because that's where you're choosing to direct your focus.

If you stand chatting with someone about how hard it is to lose weight, about how awful it is to struggle for so long and making no progress, and coming up with reasons and/or excuses – you are very strongly putting your focus on the exact opposite of what you want. You are reinforcing the 'fat program' every time you engage in this.

Are you beginning to see why you've been stuck for so long?

Basically, every thought you have about your weight is either taking you towards or away from your desired body. This first part of this book has been about showing you how you have been very effectively taking yourself in the opposite direction to what you really want.

When you catch yourself thinking or talking about your weight. Ask yourself "Am I taking myself towards or away from my ideal weight?"

Overweight ⬅————————➡ Slim

There is a lot coming up about how to reverse all this negative programming later in the book.

This Is Why You Haven't Lost Your Weight Yet
Next time you wonder why you can't lose weight – look at all these things you're regularly doing to keep your weight exactly where it is.

- Pitching will power (dieting) against your powerful subconscious and established habits
- Not realising that a change in mind-set is a prerequisite for your life-long ideal weight
- Not realising you have to become a slim person in your mind before it happens to your body – you have to go there in your mind first and then your body will follow
- You didn't understand the cycle of change
- You hadn't decided on a weight loss goal that was so good that it would see through the inevitable trough in the cycle of change
- You continually program your powerful subconscious to keep you fat by where you chose to direct your focus
    - Your 'fat chat' with friends and/or work colleagues
    - Your 'fat defending' of your current position
    - Your excuses for being overweight
    - Your negative criticism and feelings about yourself and your weight
    - Disliking and feeling jealous on seeing a slim

person
- Feeling hard done by that all your effort never seems to work
- Looking for reasons why you can't succeed
- Worrying about how you look
- Worrying about how you weight is affecting your health

As you become convinced that weight loss is indeed all in the mind, it will become increasingly obvious to you as to why you haven't succeeded yet.

Now you've got an insight into what you've been doing wrong (through little or no fault of your own I hasten to add), let's make a start on doing things differently. And doing things differently will get you a different result, which is definitely what you want!

Part 2
Changing Your Thoughts To Lose Your Weight

Part 2
Changing Your Thoughts To Lose Your Weight

In the previous section, I introduced to you how important your everyday thoughts are to your health and weight. I'm going to take that further now, because when this starts falling into place weight loss gets easier and easier.

You no doubt have lots of thoughts about yourself as you go through your day. Every thought you have about your weight takes you in one of two directions – either towards being overweight or towards being slimmer. You have to know what 'slim' means for you so your subconscious mind has something to hook onto, and ultimately deliver for you.

Overweight ←————————————→ Slim

Imagine that you could put all your thoughts, comments, conversations, feelings, and observations about weight related things into two buckets – one for everything that's focused on 'fat', and the other for everything that's focused on 'slim' (or whatever that means for you). Put them into opposing sides of a scale. What would be the result?

Thought bubbles on unbalanced scales:
- I can't lose weight
- Look at me, I'm so fat
- Nothing ever works for me
- Nothing fits me
- I'm really looking foward to feeling healthier
- I look nice even though I'm not as slim as I'd like to be

Every thought regarding your weight has an impact because your subconscious is always listening and using those thoughts to either reinforce an existing program (making it stronger) or beginning to lay down a new program (a slimmer one).

To lay down a new program (which will make the old one redundant), you need to know exactly what you want it to do and think in alignment with it. A must in this process is gradually reducing your attachment to the old program, which feels a little tough at first because this is something new. It's just like when you first learned to drive, but you did that didn't you? And if you didn't do that you no doubt learned how to do other things that were just as complex.

7. Accepting Where You Are

It might feel counterintuitive to accept where you are right now with your weight. Some people worry if they accept where they are they won't change. Not so, in fact, it's the exact opposite.

If you don't accept where you are with your weight right now, it means your everyday focus will be on your weight as it is now, which is exactly what you don't want! This sets up a BIG resistance to any movement forward with your weight loss because you can only end up getting what you give your predominant focus to.

Your non-acceptance of where you are right now shows itself constantly throughout the day.

It might be when you see a photo of yourself or look at yourself in a mirror and say to yourself "I'm fat" and then feel horrible about it. Your focus is on being overweight which means you're going to keep getting more of the same.

Your 'fat chat' with friends is non-acceptance, as is any 'fat defending' or excuses/reasons for not changing. These all act as a ball and chain around your ankle – too many of these and you're at a standstill, or getting fatter as time goes on because they are pulling you backwards.

What do *you* think about or say when it comes to *your* weight? What 5 things did you write down in the first section of this book? It's important you start noticing this. What's the knock on effect of that on how you feel about yourself? How are you making yourself feel? Notice this too. Just how bad have you been making yourself feel?

It's time to change.

I'd like you to practice accepting where you are with your weight by saying "I am where I am" often!

This might feel odd at first, like clasping your hands the 'wrong' way. Try that again now to remind yourself. It's not wrong, it's just different.

Accepting where you are shifts you towards neutral ground and this allows you to begin looking in the other direction, i.e. where you want to go.

Your new mantra will sound something like "I am where I am, and I am looking forward to _____" (whatever that is for you).

Try that and see how it makes you feel. Compare that feeling to the feeling you create when you think the things on your list. What difference do you notice?

You've got to start directing your thoughts towards what you actually want if you want something different. This probably means most of your thoughts need to be pretty much the opposite of what they have been.

At first, your old thoughts will continually pop into your mind because this is your current habit. This is the program you've got running right now. When this happens **you have the choice** of correcting the old with the new.

Looking at yourself in the mirror and deciding you don't particularly like what you see and not feeling happy about that, is fine at first. It's only by experiencing what you don't want, that you realise you want something different.

It's at this point things tend to go wrong for most people because they don't take the next step of clearly defining what they do want and focusing on that instead. What they do is continue to bang the drum of what they don't want, keeping their focus firmly fixed on where they are.

You get what you focus on. If you continue to be 'fat focused', by disliking your body as it is, talking about it to your friends, and feeling unhappy about it - you get more 'fat'.

When the thought "I hate being overweight" pops into your head out of habit, you have the opportunity to build your new program by quickly correcting it. This thought needs neutralising and you do that easily by saying "I am where I am right now, but I'm doing something new and I'm looking forward to _____."

Just how easy is that to do?

The trouble with things that are so easy to do is that they are equally easy not to do! Every time you don't correct thoughts like this you are wasting the brilliant opportunity to take one of your shackles off. Whereas every time you take just *5 seconds* or less to correct, you remove one.

It's just 5 seconds. You've got time and energy for that! If you haven't, you haven't aimed yourself at something you really want yet.

By accepting where you are, deciding *clearly* what you want instead, accepting there's a distance to travel to get there, you take your focus away from what you don't want, and put it on what you do want.

This is your starting point to lay down your new program.

8. What Do You Want?

Have you got really clear about it? How happy does it make you feel when you think about it?

When patients or coaching clients complain about their weight I ask them what they want instead. Often the answer is either slow in coming (because they've not really thought about it and therefore don't know what they want), or is some variation of "I don't want to be overweight" (which is hardly inspiring and not going to get them through the cycle of change).

What do you want?

If you can't answer this immediately and spit it out without hesitation, you don't really know what you want yet. You've got some thinking to do.

If your face doesn't light up when you say or think about what you want, then you haven't aimed at the right thing yet. Again, you got some more thinking to do.

If you've put a deadline on being 'slim' you've built in a gremlin which will probably sabotage your efforts. You can't put a timeframe on something you haven't successfully done before because you don't know what it is. To date, you haven't lost your weight in a way that's enabled you to keep it off long term and never look back.

Timeframes build in pressure and worry. This builds in 'fat focus' – "what if I'm still fat for the wedding and look horrible in the photos?"

Your subconscious is 'inclusive'. This means that whatever has your conscious attention is fed back to your subconscious as something that you want in your life. So if you say you don't want to be overweight (for the wedding, holiday whatever it is for you), your attention is actually on being overweight. Your subconscious gets the message you want to be overweight because that's where you're placing your attention and your subconscious is inclusive. That's the way your subconscious works, it's *not the same* as your conscious mind.

The louder you shout "NO" at something, the stronger the message is to your subconscious that you want this thing you're shouting no at.

The only way to exclude things from being fed back and programmed into your subconscious is by giving them *no attention* at all. The more you say you don't want something, and the stronger your feelings are about this thing you don't want - it results in great attention to this unwanted thing. Because of the *inclusiveness* of your subconscious, you're going to keep getting this unwanted thing or get even more of it.

You exclude things by redirecting your focus to what you actually want.

To your conscious mind these two statements might mean the same thing:

- I don't want to be fat
- I want to be slim

But to your subconscious, they mean exactly the opposite to each other. One statement is giving attention and focus to 'fat', the other to 'slim'.

So your *number one job* is defining exactly what you want and putting your attention mainly on that, rather than continuing to bang the drum about what you don't want.

You need to begin training yourself to think differently, to think about what you want instead of what you don't want. This may feel unnatural at first, just like joining your hands together the 'wrong' way.

With practice, you will gradually remove your attention from unwanted things as you place more and more attention towards what you want. It will take practice in the beginning because you've probably spent years training yourself to focus on what you don't actually want. It's become a habit, which is one of the big reasons you've been struggling to lose weight for a long time.

Are you clear about what you really want yet?

You need to be clear, because when you are you can engage a really powerful part of your subconscious mind, the reticular activating system (RAS).

9. The Reticular Activating System

Your RAS is the goal-seeking part of your mind. When it has been programmed it's like a sniffer dog searching for drugs, it just doesn't stop until it's found some. The energy to pursue the goal seems boundless!

Your RAS is part of your subconscious mind which means you're not aware of what it's doing until it presents something to your conscious mind. Even though you're not aware of it, it is working the whole time to help you achieve the goals you've programmed into it. You've successfully programmed lots of goals before, sometimes deliberately, more often accidently.

Have you ever bought a car?

Part of your decision-making process might have been to test drive a particular car, to make sure you really want it. Once you've had the test drive, you've seen the car and really like the look of it, you've heard the sounds of the engine running and the doors closing, you may have noticed it smells different to your current car. You've felt what it feels like to drive. You may say something to yourself like "I want this car!" and feel really happy about the thought of having it. You imagine it being yours even though you're still driving your old one for the time being.

As you absorb enough information about this car, you start to feel happy about your decision and realise you really do want this car. The thought of having this car and driving it is making you feel good, excited even if cars are your thing.

You don't have this car yet, but you're looking forward to having it at some point.

And then a funny thing happens.

Prior to deciding you wanted this particular car, you hadn't noticed many on the road, and now all of a sudden they seem to be everywhere! Especially in the colour you like. They just keep popping up all over the place!

Has it just happened that there are all these cars on

the road all of a sudden? Or were they there before? They were there before, but you didn't notice them because you hadn't *made them relevant* to your RAS. But you made them relevant by communicating your desire to own this car to you RAS. You did that by focusing on what you want and having feelings about it, in this case, good feelings.

Emotion attached to focus is the way your subconscious hears your message.

Your RAS is constantly filtering absolutely masses of information that is constantly around you. Only the information that is relevant, because it has been programmed into your RAS (like the smell of cocaine into a sniffer dog), will be caught in the filter and then it is presented to your conscious mind "oh look, there's another one of those cars I really like!" Your RAS has picked it out and shown it to you.

This is a really simple example of how you successfully program your RAS with something you want. You've been specific about what you want, you've 'tried it on' by test driving the car, and most importantly you've felt good about it. You know what it looks like, sounds like, feels like, and the thought of having it makes you feel good.

Have you done this kind of thing regarding your weight loss goal? Probably not, because most people don't. But what would happen if you did?

Let's pretend you've decided exactly what you want and you've 'tried it on for size' in your imagination. Remember, your subconscious responds in the same way to vividly imagined things as it does to real life. So it *doesn't matter* that you can't 'test drive' your new body in real life before you've actually got it.

You've communicated your desire of the new slim you to your RAS and the vast majority of its work is going to be happening below your consciousness, so you won't know what's going on. But what can you expect to happen?

Seemingly odd things begin to happen when you get this right, which can sometimes leave you feeling surprised and even a little confused:

- You notice you're full before your plate is empty and stop eating. You're happy saving the food for another time
- You decline pudding, without feeling hard done by
- You find yourself walking instead of driving, and even enjoying it!

- You are more often drawn to healthier food options and don't feel left out looking at your friends eating cake
- You say no to the cake that you always have in your favourite café, and feel ok about that because you can have it if you want it
- Other times you choose to have the cake and enjoy it without feeling bad
- Instead of eating in response to stress you deal with it in a healthier way

This stuff starts to happen without willpower. Think about that for a moment. Just how good will that be? This is the power at your fingertips when you engage your subconscious mind on purpose, rather than by accident. And you won't be doing anything you haven't done before. You just haven't done it for your weight... yet.

10. You Can't Hit Anything Unless You Take Aim

What are you aiming at? You need to know this because if you don't have a target, it's going to be like shooting an arrow with a bow with a blindfold on. It's not going to end well, is it?

Let's say it's time for a holiday and you fancy going somewhere warm, sunny and relaxing. You pop into the travel agent and say "I'd like to go somewhere warm, sunny and relaxing, please."

If you don't give any other information about what you want, the agent can't help you. She'll either do nothing until you fill in the gaps, so you stay where you are. Or she sends you to her best guess – you could end up in a tent on the outskirts of the Sahara desert. Perhaps it's not a good idea to leave this to chance. Maybe you need to decide exactly what it is you want to do!

Where do you want to go? There are loads of places that could fit the bill. You could go to Florida, Spain or Greece. You have to be specific about what you want if the travel agent is going to make this happen for you.

You decide Portugal sounds nice because it will be

warm and sunny. Not only can you relax but you can enjoy good food, chill out by the sea, and choose some really nice accommodation (because camping isn't your thing).

You've decided what you want.

You've done all this in your mind's eye. Even though you're sat at home and the weather might be miserable, or you're sat at work and not particularly enjoying yourself – what's happening right now doesn't stop you looking forward to a holiday and then taking action to make it happen.

When you know where you want to go and you

really want to go there, you make a plan and make it happen. Obstacles and irritations along the way are dealt with because you know what you want and you really want to get there.

Once you've decided what you want, you can think about the steps you need to take to get yourself there – but not before.

If you start taking steps before you know where you're going - where are you going to end up! This is what you do when you go on a diet, because if you really knew where you wanted to go and communicated that with your subconscious mind – *a restrictive diet for the rest of your life would not be in your plan.* Unless you want to be miserable or end up piling all the weight back on when you caved in and stopped the diet.

There are lots of steps to take to reach your holiday, like booking time off work, holiday shopping, booking flights, hiring a car and lots more. But you can't make a concrete plan until you know where you're going.

You know where you're going, you can see it in your mind's eye and you're looking forward to it so much that all irritations and potential obstacles become manageable and just things to get done – like the organising before you go and the travel delays. You get through all of this because you know where you're going and you know it's going to be great when you get there!

In summary, this is what you've done:
Destination = I'm enjoying a relaxing holiday with my family in the Algarve in an all-inclusive hotel overlooking the beach.

You've decided what you want and have been really clear about this. That means you were able to make a plan.

Plan:
- Book time off work
- Book the holiday with the travel agent
- Book car parking at the airport
- Organise a hire car
- Go shopping
- Pack

There is quite a lot you've gone through to make this trip happen.

How much thought and detail did you go into the last time you tried to lose weight?

In the first section, I asked you to write down what you wanted. If you came up with something, that's great. If you sat and thought about it but didn't come up with anything, that's ok too. The only bad thing is if you didn't even stop and think about it and just kept reading. You have to consider, are you really serious about losing weight? Or are you just reading this to fool yourself into thinking you're taking action?

You may have realised you don't know what you really want when it comes to your weight loss. How does that feel? Surprising, irritating, confusing or annoying? But realising you don't know what you want is a really good start!

You MUST nail this bit of the process because you can't hit anything unless you take aim. And you need something to draw you in when you're in the bottom of the trough in the cycle of change.

If you're like most people your weight loss aim is going to need a rework to make it an effective foundation for your weight loss plan. Otherwise, you're going to be building on sand and any success you have won't last long.

11. The 'How To' Is Not Important At The Beginning

While you're deciding what it is you want you must push all thoughts of 'how to do it' out of your mind. Because the fact is, at this point you don't know how to do it (otherwise you would have done it already and not be reading this book).

If you don't know how to do it, there is a temptation for your mind to shut down and come to the conclusion that it can't be done. This is a massive road block that an awful lot of people never get past. You'll find yourself thinking or saying things like:

- Nothing works for me
- I've tried everything and nothing has worked
- I like my food too much to lose weight
- I've got no motivation

These are all statements indicating that you don't know how to do it. But instead of accepting that you need more information and help, you're going with what you already know and making the assumption it can't be done (from your current limited knowledge).

When really unhelpful things like this pop into your head (and they will), treat them like interrupting and noisy little children. Ask them to politely shut up for the time being, because you're looking at something new and they can't help you, as they have no knowledge of it.

Speaking of young kids, they are an awful lot better at this kind of thing than most adults. You can ask a kid what they want to do when they grow up and they may come out with something like "I want to be an astronaut". As they say it, their face lights up because at that moment they're imagining being an astronaut. They are an astronaut!

They're not bothered about the 'how to' or what anybody else thinks. They just answer the question without letting the 'how to' get in the way. You get an honest answer that's not edited because they don't know how to achieve it at that point. They just go to what they want in their mind.

No 'how to' obstacles get in the way to kill their dream.

When you've decided what you want and *communicated that to your subconscious,* you will begin to get the feeling of "I can do this! I don't know quite how yet, but I can do this!" You get that feeling because *you can do it.*

You need the power of your subconscious to take this journey, so you have to shut the 'non-believers' up (your negative and critical self-talk). The 'non-believers' are working on past experience and the knowledge you have up to now. They are not aware of the new knowledge yet and with new knowledge you can do new things! You need to shut them up long enough for your new ideas about yourself to gain traction.

Thinking about the 'how to' too early, i.e. before you've become clear about what you want, kills off your dreams before you can even properly think about them. Here are a few examples of that in action:

- I want to get into my size 10 jeans again, but I can't see that happening because I've been trying for years!

- I'd love to be fit enough to dance again, but effort will be too much and I haven't got the motivation these days and besides, my knees are sore
- I'd love to be thin, but I've been fat all my life and I can't realistically see that changing.

When you think about what you want and a 'yeah but' rears its head, it's time to stop that right now! Because it will kill off your dream and you won't go anywhere.

You start thinking about the 'how to' AFTER you've decided what you want, not at the same time or before.

12. Getting Clear About What You Want

I'm going to give you some real examples from people I've worked with to help lose weight, starting with the first attempts (and explaining why they will fail) and working up to a clearly decided goal that puts the foundation down for successful weight loss.

Each time I asked, "In terms of your health and weight what to you want?"

"I don't want to be fat."

When your conscious mind thinks and says this, you are focused on where you are now. You're saying you don't want to be here, but where do you want to go? You're not thinking about what you want. You are allowing the here and now to distract you. Rather than saying "I am where I am right now, but where do I want to go from here?" your thoughts are stuck on what you have now. Your subconscious gives you what you focus on because it is inclusive. If this is your goal you're staying overweight because your focus is on 'fat'.

"I don't want to keep struggling with low energy and have sore knees."

This one is making the same mistake as the one above. Once again this person is saying what they don't want, but not saying what they do want. They are directing their focus on what they have now, so they'll stay there.

"To be lighter and fitter."

This is slightly better, but it still won't get you out of the starting blocks. You haven't identified with this goal by saying "I am lighter and fitter". When you make a decision you tend to take ownership of it:
- I am going on holiday
- I am buying a new car

"To be lighter and fitter" is like a limp bit of celery, it's got no substance at all. There's no firm decision behind it.

Also – 'lighter and fitter' is the equivalent of going to 'warm and sunny' for your holiday. Where is it? You haven't decided where you're going, it's just vague and woolly and it gives your subconscious nothing to work with. Your RAS hasn't been given anything to hone in on, so it can't take you anywhere.

"I am wearing my favourite clothes and they fit me. I

like what I see in the mirror."

This one is really getting somewhere. This is like thinking about a holiday and knowing exactly where you're going. You have identified with what you want by using 'I'. You are taking ownership of this. You have answered the question simply and clearly. You have clothes in your wardrobe that you intend to look good in again.

Notice there is no negative focus there. The only thing getting fed back to the subconscious with this goal is 'clothes fit and I like what I see'. This implies weight loss and being happy. This is the kind of thing you're aiming for.

The other thing to notice about this one is it's stated in the present as if it's happening now. Your subconscious is present-focused, so this will work well.

So it's time for your next attempt, write it here.

Why do I want to lose weight?

Now you're getting clearer about what you want, it's time to start injecting a bit of power into it.

Think about something coming up that you're looking forward to, it might be a holiday or a night out. Imagine what it will be like and the enjoyment you'll have. When you do this, you feel nice and you look forward to it and are drawn to it all the more aren't you?

Try the same thing with your weight loss goal. Close your eyes and imagine you've reached it:
- What do you see – how good do you look?
- What do you hear – imagine someone special saying how great you look
- How does it feel – how is your body moving and feeling? What new things are you doing as a result of your weight loss?

Don't skip over this bit. Literally 'try this on' in your imagination because you need to check that you're happy with it and that it makes you feel really good. It's like test driving a car, but this time you're doing this in your imagination. You've got to check you like where you're headed.

In the next section, you'll be taking this goal and

I'll be showing you how to literally add a stick of dynamite to it, to make it super effective at propelling you towards the weight loss you want. But for now, just imagine what it's like the best way you can – it will take you only a few seconds, so please do it because it's going to help you.

Only when you've imagined being at your destination (and checking that you're happy with it) are you ready to allow your mind to think a bit about the 'how to'. However, if you haven't written anything down yet and imagined what it's like to be there – please do that first, because if you don't know where you're going, how can you plan your journey to get there?

Would you turn up at the airport without a ticket?

13. The 'How To' Lose Weight

Only start this if you've made a decision about where you're going. If you start this before you know where you're going, you're arriving at the airport without knowing where you're off to. You wouldn't do that for a plane journey, so why would you do it for something as important as this?

It might be that you've written your goal down and the gap between where you are now and where you want to go is huge. If that's the case, that's absolutely brilliant because it means you didn't let the 'how to' get in the way of your decision. Well done!

Think back to the time you had never sat behind the wheel of a car before. The gap between that starting point and being a competent driver seemed pretty big didn't it, but you did it.

You may not have written down all the steps you took, but you were aware of all the things you had to get to grips with and put it all together to become a competent driver.

It's the same kind of thing here, only you're going to write down your possible steps. You don't know all the answers and steps yet, so you're going to be adding to this and tweaking as you go along.

What steps do you know of right now that you could potentially take to reach your goal? Here's a possible few to get you started:

- Study this book and put into practice what I learn until I have a slim mind-set
- Make a small amount of time every day to focus my mind on reaching my goal
- Do I need to learn more about nutrition, if so, how will I do that? (Hint – my first book Living the Slim Life)
- Walk an extra 2,000 steps every day

Carry on writing your list. The more things on there the better, because it means you're thinking. It doesn't mean you have to do everything on your list, at this stage, you're kicking some ideas around. Some you'll move forward with, others you won't. Just get all your ideas written down.

It's a bit like looking across a really wide river that you need to cross. Each possible step is a stepping stone. The more stepping stones there are, the more confident you become about crossing the river. You see that you can do it. It's just matter of moving forward across the steps.

The more ideas and the better plan you have about reaching your weight loss goal, the more your confidence will grow about reaching it.

This is easy. You do the same kind of thing when you plan a holiday.

Summary
In this section, I've introduced the concept that every thought about your weight takes you in one of two directions. Either towards being slim or towards being overweight.

Overweight ◄─────────────► Slim

You need to take your attention and thoughts away from where you are right now and the things you don't want, by accepting where you are. Some people worry that by accepting where they are now, they won't want to change.

Up to now, you haven't been accepting where you are.

How has that been working out?

You've got to start doing different things if you want

a different result and some of the things I'm asking you to do may feel a little strange at first. Remember how odd it felt in the last chapter when I asked you to interlink your fingers the opposite way to normal. Different does not make it wrong, it's just different!

I've introduced you to your reticular activating system and shown you how you already use this to successfully achieve goals. I've briefly explained how you can start deliberately programming it to help you reach your weight loss target.

The programming starts by clearly deciding what you want (without worrying about how you're going to do it). This has to be presented to your subconscious in the way it understands (more about that coming up).

It's only when you've clearly decided what you want and communicated it with your RAS that you're in a position to start thinking about possible steps you can take to reach your goal. It's highly likely you don't know all of these yet, so this is going to be work in progress.
In the next section, I'm going to go deeper into programming your subconscious mind and give you practical tools to make your weight loss goal happen.

Let's get stuck in!

Part 3
6 Steps to Personal Change and Weight Loss

Part 3
6 Steps to Personal Change and Weight Loss

I find nutrition and exercise and how it comes together to create a healthy slim body, fascinating. I wrote all about that in my first book – Living the Slim Life. To put nutrition and exercise into your life in a way that improves your health and drops your excess weight, it needs to become a part of your natural everyday life. This requires a change in your thinking – and the art of doing that fascinates me even more.

When you embark on something significant or big it involves personal change. Knowing how to change and being able to do it is powerful. It's powerful because it enables you to achieve what you want in life.

The seed for my own change (and hence this book) was sown in the summer of 2015, although I didn't know it at the time. By the end of the year, I'd had three substantial emotional knocks. Because they came pretty much together, their effect on me was multiplied, rather than simply being added together.

I was at a low point in my life emotionally and I knew that being in this place I was not in a resourceful state. Therefore, I couldn't make anything significant happen or move forward with my life. However, I needed to get what I wanted.

I'm a real home bird. I love my home and I love spending time there. I love the sense of 'being at home' when I'm in it. I'd lost a lot - my Dad, my Nan and a 13-year relationship. At that point it looked like the next thing could be my home, this place I was hiding away in which made me feel safe. Due to choices I'd made in the previous 2 years there was no chance of me either keeping the home I was in, or getting another one to make my own. This seemed like too much on top of everything else.

I knew if I stayed emotionally low I would lose my home, because if I was going to stand any chance of keeping it (or having something else) I needed to get into a resource state – and I couldn't access that place feeling as low as I did.

I knew what I didn't want – to lose my home. I knew I was worrying about that and worry means I was focussing on exactly what I didn't want to happen! I also knew if I carried on like that I would bring that reality into my life.

The stronger the sense of something you don't want,

the easier it is to know what you do want. You just have to turn your head 180 degrees and look in the opposite direction. I wanted a have a nice home that I felt comfortable and safe in.

At that point I didn't know how I was going to achieve that. I couldn't see the wood for the trees with all the emotional stuff going on. Thoughts of 'how to' made me feel anxious, as if it was impossible.

Then it dawned on me – I needed to practice what I preached! I knew I had to forget the 'how to' until I was ready to look at that. I needed to take a step or two back.

I knew I couldn't achieve anything big from a low emotional state, so my starting point was to decide what I wanted. Completely forget the 'how to' for a while and to pick myself up emotionally to reach a resourceful state. Once I was feeling mentally stronger, I would figure the 'how to' out and get this sorted!

I've spoken to a lot of overweight people and I've found a lot of you are pretty low emotionally. This might be because of your weight, or it might be something else and the weight is just adding to it. But while you are emotionally low it's going to be very difficult to achieve something big. And for a lot of people achieving long-lasting weight loss is a going to be a big achievement, but so worth it.

One of the benefits to me for going through all that emotional upheaval was the opportunity it gave me to discover how quickly I could turn my mind-set around and not only get back to where I was, but far exceed it. It's been an incredible journey that I've taken myself on, which I'm still relishing.

You can use exactly the same techniques to achieve weight loss, even if you've been trying for years already. I'm going to give you my six-step plan to personal change and achievement.

14. There Is Something You Want

Going back to the cycle of change, you need to decide what success is for you, because you're going to put that into *your* cycle. A sentence or two will be fine at this point.

Before finally pulling this information into this book, I presented this material to a small group of my blog readers. One of them made a copy of this picture, wrote his 'success' on it and pinned it up where he could see it.

This would serve as a great reminder for him that it's normal to have ups and downs on a journey like this and not to be derailed by them, but instead to focus on what's important - where he's going.

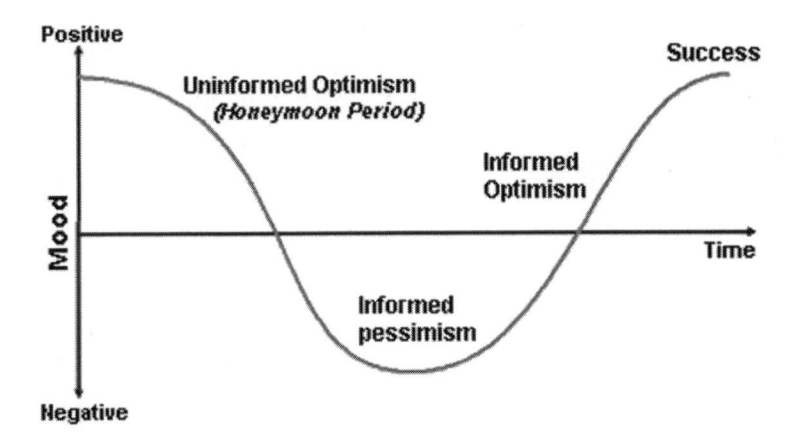

By now you really should have decided what success is for you, if you haven't – now really is the time! You need this to know where you're going and to inspire you to get out of the trough because it's normal to end up down there. I did on my cycle and I was determined to come up and out on the right side.

When I did this, I decided I wanted a home I loved that was all mine. A place I could feel great in. That was my 'success' and at the time I decided it, it seemed out of reach – so at this point, it was vital not to kill it off by not knowing the 'how to' and reaching the conclusion it was impossible.

15. Forget The 'How To' And Dream Your Dream
What is a belief?

You might believe that it's impossible for you to lose weight. Many years ago people used to believe the world was flat and that the sun circled the earth. You might believe you're not good enough. You might believe in God. You might believe money makes you happy.

You weren't born with any of these beliefs, or any of the others that you have. So what is a belief and where did they come from?

A belief is a thought that you've had enough times to believe that it's true. A lot of our beliefs are programmed into us as children by the adults around us, but as we go through life we develop others.

You might feel you *know* certain things 100%, and when you *know* something to be true, then you just know it and don't have to think about it. There's a difference between knowing something and just believing it. What do I mean by that?

Do you believe the sun will come up tomorrow, or do you know it will come up tomorrow? That's something you don't need to question or have doubts about, you just know it will come up! There's a feeling of certainty about that. It's not something you have to deliberate about or question – it's going to happen and you know it.

When you have certainty about something, for example, you're going to be on holiday next week, to a certain extent you chill out and just get on with doing the necessary to make it happen.

When you only believe something, there is room for doubt. You question it and find yourself hoping it's true, or hoping it will happen. But believing is at least a step beyond not believing, and on the right track to knowing. I'm sharing with you techniques that will get you to the point of *knowing* you can be slim IF you do them of course. Once you know you can do it, nothing will hold you back. Reaching a point of *knowing* you can do something is like installing a new blueprint into your subconscious. Your body will *have* to follow.

If you tell yourself enough times that you can't lose weight, at some point you will believe it, and worse than that you may know it! It becomes part of your subconscious programming. And then you just accept you can't lose weight.

This belief completely limits you and needs to change – but only you can change it.

If for a moment you can experiment with the idea that a belief is only a thought you keep thinking, and you have beliefs that are making you miserable and keeping you stuck. Then, wouldn't it be interesting to keep having a thought about yourself that you don't believe yet, and have it often enough that you start to believe it?

Interesting..

At the beginning of 2016, I didn't believe I could keep my lovely home, or get another remotely to my liking. I wasn't in any sort of state to make that happen.

I decided I had to make myself believe (and then know) I could achieve my 'success' before I could think about how I was going to do it. Because at that point, every time I thought about it, I would get anxious believing it wasn't possible.

I was at a really low and un-resourceful point. I could not figure out the 'how to' until I'd had developed some faith in myself that I could make it happen. At that time, because of all that had happened, I didn't have access to the mind-set I needed to get what I wanted. At present, you may not have access to the mind-set you need to lose your weight, but you can achieve that.

I suspect if you've been trying to lose weight for ages you seriously doubt you can do it. You certainly don't know that you can lose your weight and keep it off. Perhaps you don't believe you can be happy and slim at the same time. Therefore it's not going to happen. You'll keep sabotaging yourself and conforming to your current programming. Or you'll lose weight (for a while at least) and be miserable while trying to stay slim. Then get more miserable when it all piles back on again.

You need to start changing what you believe is possible for you and since we're playing with the idea that a belief is only a thought you keep thinking, this could be quite simple!

16. Changing Your Belief

I'm fully signed up to 'a belief is only a thought you keep thinking', so it was easy for me to keep thinking this thought I didn't believe! At the beginning of 2016, the type of home I wanted was out of my reach, I didn't believe I could do it. However, I knew if I put in a bit of effort I could convince myself I could do it. Once I'd done that, the 'how to' would come to me and I'd make it happen.

Is losing weight and achieving better health worth a bit of mental effort for you?

In my cycle of change, my 'success' was "I'm sitting in MY lovely house with my friends and I'm having a great time". I needed to communicate this to my subconscious mind and I took a few minutes every morning for a while to do just that.

Your subconscious works only in the present, it is inclusive (whatever you focus on it 'hears'), the more emotion attached to the thought the louder it 'hears' you. It makes no distinction to something real or something vividly imagined.

You've got what success means to you regarding your health and weight. You need to create a scenario around that, which you can call to mind in your imagination. But before you do, think about something you're looking forward to. It might be a holiday or a special night out with friends. When you imagine it, how does it appear in your imagination? Is like a miniature movie, i.e. a life-like moving image? Is it a conversation that you can imagine in your head? Or does it come to mind more by feelings?

It's useful to check in with how you imagine things naturally, because I'm going to illustrate this with how *I* do it. This way works for me, but you may need to approach it a little differently to get the best out of it for you.

Success for me was owning my home and not just any home. What I wanted was pretty specific and I needed to communicate this to my subconscious.

I turned my success of 'I'm sitting in MY lovely house with my friends and I'm having a great time' into this scenario.

I was sitting around my dinner table with seven of my favourite people. My sister would hush everyone down and then propose a toast to congratulate me on my home. We'd clink classes to celebrate.

I would see this all through my own eyes, as if I was sitting at the table looking at and hearing my friends. I would imagine it so vividly it would feel real and it would make me smile. Some dreams feel real while you're having them, don't they? That's what I was aiming for with this. That's what I want you to aim for with yours.

I imagined this over and over again, every morning. I gradually went from not believing I could pull it off, to thinking perhaps I could and then to thinking it was pretty much a done deal – even though I still didn't know how I was going to do it!

I'd learned this technique ages ago. But it was from Mr. Twenty Twenty at FreeNevillle.com that I stumbled across the best explanation of this and that's what I'm going to summarise for you now, so you can do this yourself. He calls it 'Feel It Real'.

Feeling It Real
You know how important it is to 'take aim', because without that you're pretty much going nowhere. I'm going to share with you how to create some real power out of knowing what your outcome is.

This technique strongly programs the reticular activating system in your subconscious mind, aiming it towards what you want. Once your subconscious is programmed and 'on your side', you will find yourself taking the kind of action that seemed difficult before, e.g. choosing healthier food more often, taking more exercise – and feel good about it! This might feel a bit weird when this starts to happen, but it is the power of programming your subconscious beginning to show itself.

1. Have a Clear Outcome
Your goal, or outcome, requires two qualities. It needs to be definite, i.e. what you want has to be clear. It also has to be determined by *you*. What I mean by that is that it has to be what *you* want. You lose the great power within this technique if you have an outcome to please others, rather than yourself. It's fine if you end up pleasing others too, but *you* have to come first with this.

The next thing is to create an imaginary scene that could happen after you have completed your goal, after you've achieved what you're aiming for with your health and weight loss. When you come at this from a place of having done it already, all the effort and 'hard work' is in the past, so you're not feeling any of that. In this place of having reached your goal you get to thoroughly enjoy where you are – this is important because this is what you want to communicate to your subconscious.

I've given you mine. Here are some examples to give you an idea of how to do it for weight loss. But you have to come up with your own for this to work for you.

I imagined going out for a coffee with an old friend who I haven't seen for a while. She was amazed at how good I looked now and gave me a lovely hug, saying how pleased she was to see me looking so well. I could feel her patting me on the back as she hugged me and she smelled like I always remembered, with the same perfume she'd worn for years.

I imagine completing a run with John and him giving me a high five, while saying how amazed he is at how far I've come. He can't believe I've finally beat him to the finish line. My body feels alive and energised and I can smell the warmth rising from it as I stand there taking in the view.

I am standing at the top of Mount Snowdon having walked up here under my own steam. The air smells clean and fresh and the view is spectacular. My wife puts her arm around my shoulder and tells me how proud of me she is.

I'm not keen for you to add a timescale into your goal if it's in the near future, because this often invites stress into it, which will stop you in your tracks. Inevitably you wonder whether you will achieve it and worry that you won't. This puts your focus right where you don't want it. You can do without this.

2. See Your Outcome From Your Own Eyes
When we imagine or remember things, we can do it in two ways. Let's take a night out with family for example. You could imagine this and see yourself sitting at the table with everyone else – in this case, you can see your body like you're watching a film with you in it. The other way you can imagine this is like you are actually there. This time you can't see your body because you're in it. You're seeing everyone else from your own eyes, just like you did at the time.

When you imagine your outcome, it's important to imagine it like you are seeing out of your own eyes. This means you do not see your own body in the image you are creating in your mind, because this creates emotional distance and you don't want that here.

You want to see it and experience it from your body – just like you would if it was happening for real. As if you were there, inside your body. When you imagine things, and see out of your own eyes like you are there (rather than a bystander), you feel it like its real, with all the emotion. That's just what you're looking for here, because emotion communicates with your subconscious very well.

To get even more power from your images – make them big, like they're on a huge cinema screen. Bigger images create more feeling. Make your images colourful and bright too – this also enhances the feeling.

3. Include Smell
The reason to include smell, if possible, is because it activates deep parts of the brain that help create real-feeling experiences in your mind. The more real this imagined scene feels, the more powerfully you are

programming your subconscious.

In the first example I gave, I used the smell of the friend's perfume. It could have been the smell of coffee in the coffee shop. In the second one I used the warm smell of a hot body. Maybe there was the smell of sweat too. I could have used outdoor smells here. It's your choice what you include in yours, but put one in because it really helps makes the imagined experience feel real.

In the third example, there is no mention of weight loss. There doesn't have to be because for this man to walk up Snowdon would require dramatic weight loss and an enormous improvement in health. To achieve this goal that would have had to have happened, so it's taken for granted that that happened along the way to make this 'feat' possible.

4. Include Congratulations
To do this, you need to include another person in your scene. It can be anyone.

Have someone in your scene to include physical congratulatory sensation. This could be something like a handshake, a hug or a high five. I put the clink of glasses into mine. This not only brings in another good-feeling sensation to the session (helping it to feel even more real), but it also includes a congratulatory element into your scene, increasing your sense of accomplishment. This creates good energy and increases the 'real' feeling. When I do mine, it's this bit that brings a smile to my face.

5. Do it in a Relaxed State

This bit is *really* important. Your brain produces several different types of brainwaves depending on the level of business that's going on up there. Different brain waves are better for different things.

When you're properly awake, you produce mainly beta waves. These are good for thinking and they are active when you do things like balancing your bank account and figuring things out.

When you slip into a relaxing and happy daydream your brainwaves calm and change from beta to alpha. If you're super relaxed they possibly change to theta. You produce alpha and theta brainwaves when you are in a relaxed and creative state. Your subconscious is open to new ideas when the 'questioning beta waves' have been quietened down. You communicate very well with your subconscious when you're in this state. This is the state you're aiming to be in when you do your 'feeling it real' sessions, a relaxed daydream-like state.

The reason you want to leave beta brainwaves behind for this is because they are good at figuring things out. While in this 'beta state' your mind has the tendency of putting up obstacles and barriers, as it's trying to figure out how you're going to achieve this. The 'how to' isn't important right now, in fact, it completely gets in the way of programming your mind, which is why you need to switch it off for this part by relaxing your mind.

Give yourself a little time to do this. 5 minutes will probably be enough. Give this your undivided attention for these few minutes and get the power from it. It will be SO worth it.

It's important you take these 5 minutes out on most days (repetition is vital here – just like it was when you were learning to drive). If you can't make the time to take just 5 minutes, think about the message you are sending to the deeper parts of your brain - 'This isn't important!'.

By doing it and taking those few minutes most days, you program the most powerful part of your mind and get it working in harmony with what you want. Your subconscious will make this happen for you IF you tell it what you want.

How to get into the right state of feeling it for real:

- Get comfy in a comfortable chair (but not so comfy that you drop off to sleep)
- Make sure you're warm enough. Use a blanket if the room isn't warm.
- Gradually move your attention from the outside to the inside by
    - Closing your eyes
    - Noticing your breathing. This helps you to relax
    - Slow your breathing down to a slow count of four on the in breath and six on the out breath
    - Breath deeper – let you stomach move out like you're inflating a balloon
    - This helps change to alpha and theta brainwaves
    - Do a countdown from 10 to 1 with each breath
    - Feel yourself become more relaxed with each breath
- Once your body and mind feel relaxed – begin
- Enter into your ideal scene in your imagination
- See it from your own eyes

- Really feel the congratulatory point
- Imagine it at least until you've created a really good feeling about what's going on

Have your scene written down and on your lap before you begin, so you can remind yourself what it is before you get relaxed. It's ok if you don't remember it all exactly right the first few times – the more you do it, the more you will remember it exactly how you want it to be.

While you imagine your scene, you might change things a bit to make it even better. It's good to tweak it as you go along until it's just right.

Some people like to do this either just before getting up out of bed or just before going to sleep. Find what time works best for you.

Troubleshooting
If you're having trouble visualising your scene (and by that I mean seeing the pictures inside your mind), imagine being in a cinema and your scene is playing out on the screen. Then literally step into it.

Some people find it hard to bring pictures into their imagination. This is where it can help to notice what you already do when you're imagining or remembering things. One of these two techniques will help you get there.

- Begin your scene with hearing a conversation with someone. You are perhaps talking about how you lost all the weight, or how good you look now. As you hear the conversation, start filling in the visuals and other elements. If the conversation on its own is enough to make you feel great, and you don't tend to think in pictures and images, then keeping it at this is fine.
- If this doesn't work, begin your scene with feeling something, perhaps how good your body is feeling now you're healthy and slim. Or the hug from the person who is in the scene with you. Then build the pictures and sounds around that.

Summary

I really can't emphasise enough just how important this process is. When you program your subconscious mind by regularly communicating with it what you want, you make this journey so much easier on yourself. You might even be making the seemingly impossible, possible just by doing this.

Without engaging your subconscious, it's possible you won't succeed at all. At the very least is will feel like cycling uphill, i.e. hard work. And it might end up being miserable when you get there because you're in contradiction to your blueprint (because you haven't changed it) and things are just not sitting well because of that.

By engaging your subconscious, you make it not only highly possible to succeed (where you may have failed loads of times before), but potentially quite easy. You'll be amazed at just how much easier things become when you get this bit right. Rather than the hard work of cycling uphill, it will feel like free-wheeling downhill.

Do yourself a favour and do this bit!

17. If You're Low You Need To Get Happier

I did something else alongside this, because as I was getting myself to the 'believing it could happen' point, I also knew I'd be even more resourceful if I were happy. Also, I wasn't enjoying being a misery. I wanted to feel happy again! Life is short. I wanted to be living mine happily.

If for whatever reason you're feeling really unhappy, you'll reach success so much easier if you work on getting yourself happier. It will also be a lot more fun!

I wrote a quick and easy plan on a piece of paper and kept it on my pillow – to remind me to do it until it became my habit.

Here it is.

> **My plan to get happy**
>
> - Begin the day looking for a handful of positive things in my life
> - Today I will look for reasons to feel good
> - As I move through my day I will look for reasons to laugh and have fun
> - Bedtime – recall the pleasant things that have happened today (and write them down)
>
> NOTHING IS MORE IMPORTANT THAN FEELING GOOD!

I wouldn't let myself get out of bed until I felt positive, even if that would make me late. I wouldn't allow myself to go to sleep until I'd written some positive things down. When you actually look for them, it's surprising just how many you can find (even when you're feeling low). These can be simple things like having a comfortable bed and feeling cosy in it, having coffee with a friend, receiving a compliment, and giving a compliment.

In the beginning, it was an effort to laugh and feel good during the day. It felt like I was putting a face on and pretending, but it gradually became easier and natural.

If you're feeling low – give this a go. It's not that hard. When you repetitively do something you form a new habit. Being happy is a habit of thought which you can develop, even if that's not your default right now.

I added something else into the mix too and I definitely want you to do this next thing.

18. Adding Power Every Day To Your New Program

You're taking five minutes every day to program your reticular activating system, so now you need to direct your everyday thoughts towards that. Your everyday thoughts need to be brought into alignment with where you're intending to go, so everything is pulling in the same direction.

If you're spending a few minutes vividly imagining being slim and then letting your everyday thoughts run amok, it's like a tug of war going on. These two activities pull in the opposite direction to each other. This is why you've got to get a handle on this. You cannot allow yourself to get stuck on where you are right now. You accept that and allow yourself to move away from it.

You might not like where you are today with your weight, but you are where you are and that's all there is to it. If you don't accept that, it will act like an anchor and keep you stuck.

When you accept it and stop focusing on it, you can look at what you want instead. This reinforces the new program you're laying down.

Overweight ◄─────────────► Slim

Start working on changing your everyday thought habits, because it's the things you do repetitively on a regular basis that produce your results.

The new thoughts focus on where you want to go – thoughts about what success looks like for you. Repetitive thoughts create new beliefs about what you are capable of.

Having new and positive thoughts about yourself, when you've had years of thinking really bad stuff about yourself can feel strange, weird and downright wrong to begin with. When it feels strange, clasp your hands together and then do it the other way to remind yourself that different does not mean wrong!

Steer your thoughts to the right track again. This can feel tough at first, like trying to steer a shopping trolley that has wonky wheels.

With the wonky shopping trolley you know you want to get around the supermarket to the checkout and get your stuff in the car. Because you know what you want, you keep it on track and do it.

It's the same kind of thing when you're cultivating new thoughts (and you're doing this because you want new results). However, unlike the wonky shopping trolley, having new thoughts gets easier the more you practice it because you're training yourself to do something different (just like you did when you learned to drive). At some point, it will become your new habit.

After a short while of keeping the 'wonky shopping trolley' (your thoughts) in line, you create a new path in your mind.

Meanwhile, the old path (the 'I'm fat thoughts') gets overgrown through lack of use.

Different thoughts create different feelings.

Different feelings about yourself create different results.

Decide what you want to think instead of all the rubbish, so when you notice a 'fat thought' coming in you can quickly change it. Effectively you're saying to your mind 'not this anymore, but this instead'.

For example, you might be holding onto a negative

thought like "I'm fat and I'll always be fat, nothing works for me". A thought like this is a drain on your energy. If you have a lot of these over the course of the day you're going to drain your energy reserves – most people's everyday thoughts expend their energy. You'll also make yourself feel horrible and reinforce a belief that is keeping you stuck.

However, when you notice yourself having a thought like this you've now got the choice to change it and that's important, because every thought you have either takes you towards where you want to go, or away from it. So you can make the choice in that moment about the direction you're going.

And it really is a choice – your choice!
Are you going in 'fat direction' by holding on to that thought? Or are you going to look in the opposite direction and correct it by saying something like:

- I am where I am today and that's ok. I'm looking forward to...
- I wonder what it's going to be like when I'm slimmer? What new things will I do?
- Won't it be great when people start noticing I'm losing weight!
- How good will I feel when I'm in that dress??

Think anything you like, as long as it's towards where you want to go! These kind of thoughts will actually give your energy a boost. For some reason, we're not in the habit of thinking good things about ourselves, but when you start doing this you are going to completely change how you feel.

If you say something bad about yourself your energy drops. If someone else says something bad about you, the same thing happens.

On the other hand, think about the little boost you get when someone says something nice to you. You can do this to yourself all day long, increasing your energy as you go along.

Most of the time we deplete our energy with the negative self-talk we have and wonder why we're tired! When you get into the habit of only tolerating the good stuff, you'll be pretty surprised at the change in your energy levels.

Negative Thought ⊖

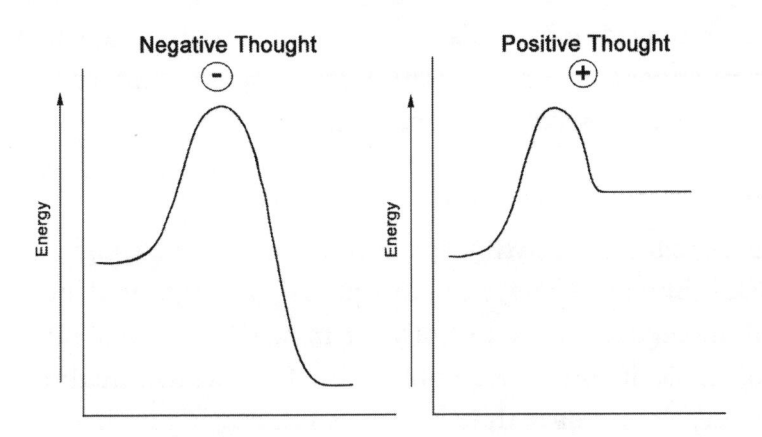

Positive Thought ⊕

(y-axis: Energy)

Stop all 'fat chat' because this is helping to keep your focus on where you are now and keeping you stuck.

I decided to shut up about my emotional upheaval after a few weeks, or at least not talk about it in negative terms. If anyone said they felt sorry for me, I'd ask them not to, because there was no need. What had happened had happened. It was done and in the past. But it had opened up new opportunities for me and I directed the conversation away from what had happened and towards the new things I was thinking and working to achieve.

It's time for you to make a choice about what you really want when the people around you start their 'fat chat'. Do you still want to be having the same conversation this time next year, or would you like to have moved on? That's the choice you're making when you choose whether to join in with the 'fat chat' or let them get on with it without you.

If you truly want something different you have to accept full responsibility for your health and weight. The time for excuses about not losing weight is done. If an excuse comes out of your mouth, and it will out of habit, if you've been doing this for a while, laugh at yourself and say "that's a bad habit rearing its head! But I'm moving on from that now".

If you've felt resentful towards slim people you have to change that, because you're not going to turn into something you resent. Instead of pointing and saying "look at that skinny cow", step back and find some inspiration from her. Ask yourself "I wonder what she's doing that I'm not. What could I learn from her I wonder?".

19. Making A Plan

Because I was determined to sort myself out and get what I wanted asap, I employed a really simple technique to make sure I was doing what needed to be done, and not kid myself I was doing stuff, when in fact I wasn't. There was no way I was letting myself off the hook with this. I wasn't going to allow myself to forget to do my 'homework' either.

I made a rolling four weekly plan. I knew I needed to convince myself I could own my own lovely home. I knew I needed to be happy to make this happen and I knew I'd have to work on my mind-set every day due to the low point I was starting at. So I made a simple chart that I ticked off as the days went on.

I knew at some point during this rolling plan I'd have my 'problem' solved and know how I was going to keep a nice home.

Beyond the initial four-week plan, I'd make a new one. But on my first plan, the most important task was a daily 'feeling it real session' – that was my priority. But I put other things on there too. The feeling it real session is always included in my four-week plans, but the other things change depending on what I feel needs to be added or taken out to get me where I'm going.

As far as you and your weight loss are concerned, I'd suggest you make a chart like this one and have 28 rows on it.

Feel It Real	Correcting thoughts	Nutrition change	Activity challenge

Definitely put 'feel it real' on there. I'd encourage you to put 'correcting thoughts' on there too. Even though this book has not dealt with nutrition and exercise, my guess is you already know what you could be doing better. What's the one big thing nutrition-wise you could start doing? What one activity related activity could you do?

You don't have to tick absolutely every single box. So if you miss a day or two, this is no reason at all to stop. You just pick it up again and get on with it. Because you are done with excuses now, aren't you?

Summary

This section of the book has given you the fairly simple tools that can dramatically change the results you are getting. You've got what you need to literally transform your health and what you see in the mirror.

All you need to do is:

- Decide what you want
- Forget about the 'how to' at the beginning
- Imagine yourself slim by 'feeling it real'
- Be happy – easier than you may think
- Change your everyday thoughts
- Make your plan (and stick to it!)

You will NEVER need a diet again when you've learned this little lot.

Closing Thoughts
It's Time to Stop Procrastinating And Make Yourself Worth It

Have you decided to lose weight now? Or are you still putting it off until next Monday or some indeterminate time in the future?

Is it still something you think you're going to do, but not yet because it's; not a good time, you're busy, you're going on holiday soon, life is a bit stressful at the moment, blah blah blah.

Did losing weight make it to your New Year's resolution this year, maybe last year too?

Most people who are overweight know the excess pounds are damaging their health. You may be easing the worry by saying that you will do something about it, just not right now, but you will!

This is a brilliant way to put things off and at the same time reassure yourself that you will get around to doing something about it – just not right now. It eases the niggling worry for a little while.

But in reality, you're kidding yourself. You play this

kind of procrastination game with yourself all the time to make yourself feel better.

"I will lose weight and get healthier, but not just now" pacifies the worry temporarily.

You could decide to lose weight now, i.e. start right now. But you feel like next week might be better. But actually today is a week on from last week and you might have put it off then.

Why do you think you'll be any different this time next week, or next month? This is like having your start date on the end of a stick and as you step forward into another week, your start date is at the end of the same stick and is pushed into the next week, you never actually reach it.

This way of thinking becomes a habit. All you have to do to see if you've developed this habit is look back and see if this is what you've been doing for a long time.

If losing weight repetitively features on the New Year's resolutions list – you're guilty of this!

Another habit people get into which stops them

deciding to lose weight now is to always look for reasons to put it off:

I'll do it when life is less stressful

There's no point starting before my holiday

I'll start next Monday

While you're playing these pacifying games with yourself the extra weight you're carrying is causing damage to your body. You might be showing signs of this already. Add time to the mix (because you keep putting it off) and the damage accumulates – you get sick, or sicker.

To start breaking out of this begin to notice the games you're playing with yourself because sometimes simply becoming aware of what you're doing can be enough to snap you out of it.

How are you putting it off? How are you kidding yourself that you will do something about it, someday?

Maybe you think it won't happen to you. Most people think like this and it's another game we play with ourselves. I hear this a lot when I'm handing out the tissues to patients who've just heard some bad news about their health. You can make a decision to lose weight now and for this not to be you.

You keep saying you want to change and get healthy, but you can't seem to summon the motivation to lose weight. You are just not doing it, even though you've been thinking you should for quite a long time.

What's stopping you?

If your health were a priority, you would find a way to lose your weight no matter what. I've seen this happen.

If you're still not changing, the fact is it's not a priority for you. The question is – will it ever be? I feel quite justified in phrasing it like that because I see people's health falling apart at the seams in my work as a doctor, and yet they still don't have the motivation to lose weight and change their ways.

Health often takes a back seat to everything else that is going on in life. But I think this 'excuse' is often a cover for something much more deep rooted and unspoken of and it comes down to self-worth.

There are a lot of people who will bend over backward to help others, often to their own detriment. But when it comes to themselves, they do very little.

They feel other people are worth their time and effort, but when it comes to themselves, it's a totally different story.

If this is you – why aren't you worth your own best effort, but everyone else is?

Do you look at the people you care about and think "don't bother looking after yourself love because you ain't worth it and no one's going to miss you if you pop your clogs early".

Do you think people look at you and think that?

When you're questioning why you aren't doing something that clearly you need to do, sometimes you have to look deeper to find out what's really holding you back.

I've come across a lot of people who don't rate themselves very highly. They might not even like themselves very much, even if what they present to the outside world is something quite different.

If this is you, on a deeper level you may have come to the conclusion you're just not worth the effort, your self-esteem is that low. You may struggle to find the motivation to lose weight until you sort this out.

You have to make yourself worth it, worth the effort and it's going to take to change.

Sometimes you need to take a step or two backward, before you can successfully move forwards. What I mean in this context is that if you have a really low opinion of yourself, that needs to change before you can confidently walk up to the starting line of your weight loss journey.

When you know you are worth it, you will find a way and you will do it – because you're worth it!

'Feeling worth it' vs. 'not feeling worth it' is pure and simply a state of mind and nothing more. Your state of mind comes from the thoughts you think and the thoughts you think can change.

What is it going to take for you to finally turn around and say "***k this! I AM worth it!" and at last find the inspiration to start your journey and give yourself the greatest gift – your best attention to you and your well-being.

One of the beauties of doing this is that you can give even more to the people around you who you love.

If you work with this book rather than just read it, you will be empowered to step up to the starting line and then finish the journey by losing your weight and keeping it off.

It all comes down to choice and that choice is yours.

What are you going to do?

Just less than twelve months ago I thought I may lose my home, and if I had done nothing with my mind-set I would have, there are no two ways about that. I wanted to be in a much better place emotionally, and still in my house. At the time this is going to print I am literally adding this paragraph last minute because I've just got the news that I've pulled it off and will be staying exactly where I want to be, at home.

This time next year where are you going to be with the things that are important to you?

About Dr. Julie Coffey and Uber Health Blog

I'm Julie Coffey and I would like to thank you for reading this book.

I am a doctor working within the NHS in the UK. I'm a General Practitioner and I qualified as a doctor in 1994. I have been working as a GP since 1998. I work mainly in Sheffield.

From an early age, I wanted to do something worthwhile. I trained as a doctor because I wanted to learn and I wanted to help people.

I've always been interested in health, but I began to find the medical community's approach to health and wellbeing increasingly frustrating. The predominant focus on treating and managing illness was to supply pills, with little emphasis on maintaining or regaining natural vitality.

When it comes to weight loss, the limit of many doctors' advice to patients was to eat less and do more. This, coupled with the pressure of body image through the media, led me to see many people continuing to destroy their health from years of following bad advice, or by continuing with diets.

In my mid to late thirties, I started to develop osteoarthritis in my knees. I knew that conventional medicine had little to offer me.

I was worried about this as I'm an active person and even things like walking became quite uncomfortable at times. I wondered if I'd get to a point where I wouldn't be able to do the things I loved - like skiing.

I decided to stop worrying. Instead, I put all my energy into discovering a solution. I wasn't going give up my ability to enjoy life without a fight.

I started reading endless books and research papers and felt like I was starting my health education again, almost from scratch. There was so much I didn't know. I found this new knowledge exciting and fascinating.

With my medical background, I began to design a regime for my body based on the learning I'd undertaken. I immersed myself in developing a natural health program that helped me make diet and lifestyle changes. My knees began to get better and were far more comfortable. I also lost the stubborn pounds that had been creeping up on me over a few years.

My medical background allowed me to sort fact from fiction and create a change in my own lifestyle. The effects were so dramatic and created such freedom for me that I was inspired to create my unique online weight-loss course 'Uber Slim', so that others could benefit from the hard work I'd done to find the answers.

So How Does My Uber Slim Program Work?
Uber Slim is all about getting back to and maintaining your natural state of health – which is good health.

Uber Slim builds on the information I've shared in this book. It gives you all the facts and structure you will need to rapidly change the way you look and feel forever, in a bite-sized way.

And on top of that, Uber Slim gives you direct access to me. This means you have your own personal coach to answer questions and help you through the tough times.

You won't find any advice here that I'm not doing myself already. And, as a doctor, I never do anything without knowing that it's the right thing for my health.

The benefit of being a doctor is that I know a lot about how the body works. I know what's happening when it goes wrong. I know what pharmaceutical drugs do. I'm also familiar with reading scientific literature and studies and interpreting them.

I only take on board lifestyle and diet changes if I'm convinced they're the right thing to do and I will get the benefits.

Through my unique Uber Slim program, you can benefit from everything I've learned, safe in the knowledge that it's coming from a highly qualified, practising health professional.

To get the benefits of Uber Slim right now, and to continue your journey, visit http://uberhealthblog.com/uber-slim-program/

You can also use the contact page to drop me an email with any questions you may have before getting involved.

It's going to be a great journey, but you have to act

now before you talk yourself out of making a positive change to your life.

Other titles by Dr Julie Coffey ...

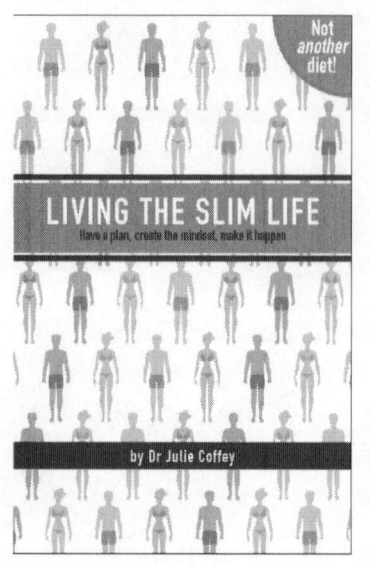

Dr Julie Coffey looks at the problem with diets and what you really need to know about nutrition. She also demystifies the whole exercise debate.

You will learn the most effective exercise techniques for weight loss and health improvement that can be done in just 20 minutes, 3-4 times a week.

You will also learn how to stay motivated and on track.

Price £11.99
352 pages
Available on Amazon in print and Kindle

NOTES ....

NOTES ....

NOTES ....

NOTES ....

NOTES ....

NOTES ....